DEAR
AMERICA

DEAR AMERICA

The Story of an Undocumented Citizen

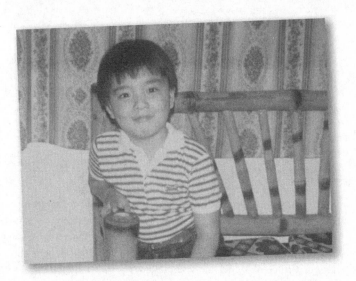

Jose Antonio Vargas

HARPER

An Imprint of HarperCollinsPublishers

Library of Congress Control Number: 2018965671
ISBN 978-0-06-291459-0
Typography by Catherine San Juan
19 20 21 22 23   PC/LSCH   10 9 8 7 6 5 4 3 2 1

First Edition

To my mother,

who sacrificed so much to give me a better life

To every teacher I've ever had,

especially the ones who taught me how to read, think, and write

America is not a land of one race or one class of men . . .
America is not bound by geographical latitudes . . .
America is in the heart . . .
—CARLOS BULOSAN

CONTENTS

INTRODUCTION

I do not know where I will be when you read this book.

As I write this, a set of creased and folded papers sits on my desk, ten pages in all, issued to me by the Department of Homeland Security. "Warrant for Arrest of Alien," reads the top right corner of the first page.

These are my first legal American papers, the first time immigration officers acknowledged my presence after arresting, detaining, then releasing me in the summer of 2014. I've been instructed to carry these documents with me wherever I go.

These papers are what immigration lawyers call an NTA, short for "Notice to Appear." It's a charging document that the government can file with an immigration court to start a "removal proceeding." I don't know when the government will file my NTA and deport me from the country I consider home.

After twenty-five years of living illegally in a country that does not consider me one of its own, this book is the closest thing I have to freedom.

1

GAMBLERS

I come from a family of gamblers.

And my future, it turned out, was their biggest gamble.

Everything about the morning I left the Philippines was rushed, bordering on panic. I was barely awake when Mama snatched me from bed and hurried me into a cab. There was no time to brush my teeth, no time to shower.

A few months prior to that morning, Mama had told me the plan: We were going to America. I would be going first, then she would follow in a few months, maybe a year at most. Until that drive to the airport, Mama and I were inseparable. We did everything together. If I wasn't at school, I was with Mama. She didn't work because she was taking care of me full-time. She made sure I was doing well at school. She cooked every meal: usually a fried egg with Spam for breakfast and, if I was good, her special spaghetti dish with chicken liver. On weekends, she dragged me to her card games and mah-jongg games. We hung out with my cousins. We visited my godmother and her family. We took trips to the province where I grew up, eating fresh mangoes from the trees and swimming in one of the many beaches and rivers with the clearest water you could imagine.

Our apartment was so tiny that we shared a bed, which was normal for people living in the city. After Papa abandoned our family when I was three years old, it was just me and Mama. I was Mama's boy.

It was still dark outside when I arrived at the Ninoy Aquino International Airport. For reasons she wouldn't explain, Mama couldn't come inside the terminal. Outside, Mama introduced me to a man she said was my uncle. In my ragtag family of blood relatives and lifelong acquaintances, everyone is either an uncle or an aunt.

After handing me a brown jacket with a "MADE IN U.S.A." label in its collar—a Christmas gift from her parents in California, the grandparents I would soon be living with—Mama said matter-of-factly, *"Baka malamig doon."* ("It might be cold there.") It was the last thing I remember her saying. I don't remember giving her a hug. I don't remember giving her a kiss. There was no time for any of that. What I do remember was the excitement of riding in an airplane for the first time.

As the Continental Airlines flight left the tarmac, I peeked outside the window. I had heard that my native Philippines, a country of over seven thousand islands, was an archipelago. I didn't really understand what that meant until I saw the clusters of islands down below, surrounded by water. So much water, embracing so many islands, swallowing me up as the airplane soared through the sky.

Whenever I think of the country I left, I think of water. As the years and decades passed, as the gulf between Mama and me grew deeper and wider, I've avoided stepping into any body of water in the country that I now call my home: the Rio Grande in Texas, not too far from where I was arrested; Lake Michigan, which touches Wisconsin, Illinois, Indiana, and Michigan, states with big cities and small towns that I've visited in the past few years; and the Atlantic and Pacific Oceans—I'm the person who goes to Miami and Hawaii without ever going to the beach.

When people think of borders and walls, they usually think of land. I think of water. It's painful to think that the same water that connects us all also divides us, dividing Mama and me.

I left the Philippines on August 1, 1993.

I was twelve years old.

2

THE WRONG COUNTRY

I thought I landed in the wrong country.

Filipino culture is fascinated with and shaped by Hollywood movies and beauty pageants. There were two television events that Mama and I watched live every year: the Academy Awards and the Miss Universe pageant. From an early age they shaped my vision of the world and of America. The America of my imagination was the America in *Pretty Woman*, *Sister Act*, and *Home Alone*. The moment I landed at the Los Angeles International Airport, I expected to see people who looked like Julia Roberts, Whoopi Goldberg, and Macaulay Culkin—people who looked like the people I watched during the Oscars. Instead, I was greeted by something like the parade of nations that kicked off the annual Miss Universe pageant, with each contestant speaking in their own tongue. The America I first encountered at the airport was a polyphonic culture that looked like and sounded like what the world was supposed to sound and look like: different people from different backgrounds speaking different languages. When I got off the airplane, I didn't feel cold or hot—it felt so new that even the air seemed different.

In the Philippines, there were two types of weather: hot and really hot. Even when it was raining, even when typhoons knocked down trees and flooded homes, including ours, I don't ever remember feeling cold. The varied weather in California—warm and sunny in the day, cool and nippy at night—required instant adjustment. I learned how to layer my clothes, and I was introduced to a thing called a sweater. I owned jackets but had no sweaters.

The bigger adjustment was living with new people: my grandparents, whom I called Lolo (Grandpa) and Lola (Grandma), and my mother's younger brother, Rolan. Until Uncle Rolan moved to the U.S. in 1991, he lived with Mama and me. Lola had visited the Philippines twice, bringing bags of Snickers and M&M's and giving relatives and friends money (one-dollar bills, five-dollar bills, sometimes ten-dollar bills) like she was an ATM. If the word "generous" were manifested in one person, it would be Lola. I only knew Lolo from photographs, where he was always posing: back straight, stomach out, chin up, the posture of someone used to being watched. He posed in front of the house, in front of his red Toyota Camry, in front of some hotel in some town called Las Vegas. I was barely three years old when Lolo moved to America. By the time I arrived in Mountain View, California, Lolo had become a naturalized U.S. citizen. He legally changed his first name from Teofilo to Ted, after Ted Danson from *Cheers*.

To celebrate my arrival, Lolo organized a party that introduced me to all the relatives I'd only heard about but never met. There were so many of them it was like we had our own little village. Among the attendees were Florie, Rosie, and David—Lolo's siblings, whom I was instructed to call "Lolo" and "Lola" as a sign of respect. Filipinos like honorifics. Everyone older than you is either a *kuya* (if he's male) or an *ate* (if she's female). Unless they are a Lolo or a Lola, you call them Uncle or Auntie, even when you're not actually related. Lola Florie, in particular, commanded respect. Lola Florie, who worked in electronics, and Lolo Bernie, her husband, who served as a U.S. Marine, owned the house that we were living in. Their two American-born sons, Kuya Bernie and Kuya Gilbert, spoke very little Tagalog, yet still managed to instantly welcome me into the family. Lola Florie was the most senior of the women in the family;

she was the reason her older brother Ted and her younger sister Rosie had been able to come to America. Lola Rosie, the loudest and friendliest of my extended family, announced that Uncle Conrad had driven seven hours just to see me in person. Uncle Conrad was a legend in our family, having escaped a life of harvesting rice and doing construction work in the Philippines to becoming an officer in the U.S. Navy, a point of pride for all of us. Standing no taller than five foot three inches and speaking English with a gravelly, guttural Tagalog accent, Uncle Conrad was in charge of 92 enlisted personnel. He was Lolo's favorite.

"Masayang masaya na kami na nandito ka na," Uncle Conrad said in front of the entire family as Lolo looked on. "We are very happy you are here."

And I was happy to be there. For the first time, I had my own bedroom, all to myself. It wasn't too big, but it was big enough for me. Lolo bought me a used fourteen-inch television set from a garage sale—I'd never had my own TV! And I'd never lived in an actual house, with a front yard and a backyard, with lemon and persimmon trees. In Manila, the teeming capital of the Philippines, the streets were loud and bustling, with street vendors selling food at every corner. In Mountain View, it was serene, flat, and quiet; the only noise I could hear was neighbors raking the leaves in their yards. In addition to raking the leaves, which was my weekly task, Lolo taught me how to use a lawn mower.

To Lolo, America was something you wear, something you buy, something you eat, and he wanted to spoil his first and only grandson—me. In the Philippines, I got to eat ice cream only on my birthday, sometimes during Christmas dinner, and to ring in the New Year. I don't think I'd consumed as much ice cream in my entire life as I did in my first few weeks and months in America. To welcome me to my new home, Lolo's way of showing his love for me and showing off America was buying a tub of Neapolitan ice cream (vanilla, strawberry, and chocolate flavors, all rolled into one) for $5.99. I must have eaten a tub a week.

Another way that Lolo showed his affection was by printing my name, using a bold, black Sharpie, on every piece of clothing I wore, most of which were the T-shirts, shorts, pants, and underwear that Lolo and Lola had purchased before I even arrived.

"Ako ang nagdala sa iyo dito," Lolo told me on the day he signed me up for school. "I brought you here." He said it in a voice that emanated pure joy and familial ownership.

I didn't have a relationship with my father. After he left our family, I saw him no more than five times in my whole life. Shortly after arriving in Mountain View, it was clear that Lolo would become the father figure I never had.

3

CRITTENDEN MIDDLE SCHOOL

"Oh, Jose, can you see?"

During my first weeks at my first American school, surrounded by my first American friends, I imagined my name was somehow in the national anthem, and I would flash a big smile whenever the whole class would sing "The Star-Spangled Banner."

"Hey," whispered my classmate Sharmand one morning when he caught me smiling while singing. "We're not talking about you." Sharmand sighed before adding, "The anthem goes, 'Oh, say, can you see.' You see?"

To say that I stood out at Crittenden Middle School is an understatement.

I loved going to school. Every day was a discovery. There was always something new to learn, whether it was the history of the Civil War or how the pyramids were built in Egypt. I joined every club I could, from the after-school yearbook club to the book club that met once a week. I made a lot of new friends, and they all looked different: black friends, white friends, friends who were Mexican, friends whose parents had come from India, Korea, and the Philippines. I was surprised how many Filipino classmates I had, but none of them spoke Tagalog. They were all born here.

I wasn't fluent in English, and I stood out for my thick Tagalog accent. Tagalog, my native tongue, was not what anyone would describe as a soft language, at least not the way I speak it. My Tagalog was all hard consonants and chopped syllables with a quick, rat-a-tat-tat sound, like the sound of tropical rain pouring down on cement. Also, the Tagalog alphabet does not have "h" and "th" sounds, which meant I struggled pronouncing a very common word like "the." So "the" in English sounds like "da" in Tagalog, and whenever I said "da" instead of "the," I stood out. One morning, when Mrs. Mitchell, the homeroom teacher, asked me to read a passage from a book out loud during class, my classmates giggled when I said "o-tor" instead of "au-thor."

I stood out because of everything I did not know.

I didn't know what kind of food was appropriate to bring

for lunch. I was the student who brought sticky rice and fried tilapia with a sauce while my classmates munched on food I'd never heard of, like peanut butter and jelly sandwiches.

"What's that nasty smell?" my classmate Sharon asked.

"It's called *patis*," I said. Fish sauce.

I didn't know how to play sports like flag football. The one time I did agree to play, I rushed to the wrong side of the field with the football in hand while my classmates, led by Sharmand, screamed, "You're going the wrong way! You're going the wrong way!"

I didn't know what *not* to talk about. When asked to talk about my favorite pet, I spoke about my dog, Rambo, the only pet I ever had. I told my classmates that Rambo was named after the Sylvester Stallone movie series, and I said that the last time I saw Rambo was hours before Mama's birthday dinner, before Rambo was killed, adoboed (the popular Filipino version of stew), and served as *pulutan*—an appetizer. My classmates were mortified. A couple of them started to cry. I later explained that, in the Philippines, dogs can serve as pets and *pulutan*—I just didn't expect it would happen to Rambo, my Rambo. I had been devastated. I assured my classmates that I did not take a bite of Rambo, that I'd never tasted a dog.

When I was growing up in Pasig, part of the capital city of Manila, whose poverty-ridden slums house four million people, dogs and cats were fed what was considered leftover food—whatever was left from lunch or dinner, usually rice;

bones from chicken, pork, or fish; skins from mangoes, bananas, guavas. I'd never heard of "pet food," never saw an aisle in a grocery store dedicated to food specifically for cats and dogs. One of my earliest memories in America was walking up and down the pet food aisle at Safeway, so transfixed and bewildered that I stopped one of the clerks. "Why does the dog food and the cat food cost more money than the people food?" I asked. The clerk answered with a long, hard glare.

America was like a class subject I'd never taken, and there was too much to learn, too much to study, too much to make sense of.

And I was excited to share everything with Mama. Long-distance phone calls were expensive. If I was lucky, I could talk to Mama once a week. Writing letters, first in longhand and later using computers at school, was cheaper. Writing letters to Mama was also a way to soothe us both, to ease the pain of our separation before we were reunited again. She was supposed to have followed me to America by now, but there was a delay in her paperwork. I had to wait some more.

On the first typewritten letter I sent Mama, written in my sixteenth month of living in America, I wrote:

What's up! How are you guys doin'? I hope all you guys are doing fine as well as I'm doing here with Lola, Lolo and Uncle Rolan. I just hate the weather here sometimes, it's too cold, I'm freezing! We even have to use the heater to keep us warm.

I wanted to show Mama that I was adapting to the language—the *what's up?—you guys—how are you doin'?* of it all. The first American student who ever spoke to me was Ryan Brown, his face covered with what I later learned were "freckles." When he greeted me by saying "What's up?" I responded, "The sky." I quickly realized that the English I spoke in the Philippines was not the same as American slang.

The letter continued:

> *It's really hard to be a 7th grader. It's like every week, we have a new project due! I'm getting crazy because my schedule is so tight. I go to school Mondays to Fridays from 7:58 a.m. to 2:24 p.m. I go to Tween Time Mondays to Fridays from 2:30–4:30. On Fridays, I go to Newsletter club after Tween Time. I walk home, eat, on Tuesdays I take out the garbage and take a two hour nap and do my homework, I have plenty of homework! As usual I joined many school clubs like Tween Time, Drama, School newsletters. I think it's really so cool that I got to use a computers a lot. In the Philippines, I didn't even had a chance to touch a computer. Here in our school, computers are everywhere! Every room there is a computer. We can't write anything without a computer!*

Over time, America had become more than a class subject I was trying to ace. America was an entire experience, and I wanted to do all of it.

It'd been more than a year since Mama and I saw each

other. I knew she was sad because I was sad. Anxious. The only way to make her happy was to make sure I didn't seem sad and to get good grades. Besides, I realized that being good at school—making friends, talking to teachers—was a way of blending in. Being accepted at school felt like being accepted in America.

Last quarter, I even got a Gold Honor Roll, I got 4.00, the perfect grade!

As a single mother, Mama leaned on her closest friends, especially my godmother, for help. The family of my godmother—her sisters, Josie and Nancy; her niece, Grace, who was like a sister to me; her mother, Elvie—was a part of our family. Over time, as I got busier at school, it became more difficult to keep in touch with everyone. I tried.

I already wrote my daily life, how about you guys!? Are you all doing fine? Every night, I always pray that may all of you be in good health. I really miss all you guys! There is nothing more important than all of you! How's Ninang [godmother]? Is she doing fine? How about Ate Grace? I heard that she's graduating next year from high school. Does she have a boyfriend now? I hope not. Tell her to please write me. How about Tita Josie, Tita Nancy and Lola Elvie? Tell them that I miss all of them and tell them that I won't ever forget them! Gotta go! I love all you very, very, very, very much!

Mama recently mailed me this letter, which I sent her more than twenty-three years ago. As I read it now, I don't recognize that young boy. What happened to all that love and longing I felt for the family and friends I'd left? Separation not only divides families; separation buries emotion, buries it so far down you can't touch it. I have not seen Mama in person since we said goodbye at the airport in 1993. Words cannot sufficiently describe how much I miss her, how painful it's been to be separated from someone who was the first person to love me and the first person I loved back. I use the word "loved" in the past tense because I don't know where that love went, if I somehow left it inside that airplane as the years and the decades passed by.

4

NOT BLACK, NOT WHITE

"You don't really look Filipino," Eleanor, the pretty girl in glasses and pigtails, was telling me. Born in the Philippines, Eleanor had emigrated to the U.S. with her family around the same time my family did.

Our arrival in Mountain View coincided with a historic change in the state's demographics. Between 1990 and 2000, the years I attended California public schools, the state's Latino and Asian populations each grew by more than a third. Meanwhile, the state's white population dropped by almost 10 percent and the black population more or less stayed the same—a statewide trend that would closely mirror the country's racial makeup in the following decades.

Crittenden Middle School was a microcosm of this irreversible shift. Like California itself, Crittenden was a minority-majority school where no single racial group had a plurality. In the early to mid-1990s, between thirteen hundred and fourteen hundred students from fifth to eighth grade attended Crittenden. About a third were Latinos, mostly Mexican; the other third were Asians, most of whom were Filipino, some Vietnamese and Indian; and the remaining third were split between white and black students. Many of the Mexicans and Filipinos were descendants of farmworkers who moved to Mountain View to work on the apricot, peach, and cherry orchards after World War II. A decade later, a Mountain View–based company called Shockley Semiconductor Laboratory developed the first silicon semiconductor devices that gave Silicon Valley its name.

Like many Filipinos in the Philippines, I grew up listening to Michael Jackson and Whitney Houston, but I didn't know Whitney and Michael were "black" or "African American." And I didn't know that Julia Roberts and Macaulay Culkin were "white." In the Philippines they were just Americans.

When it came to the subject of race, my fourteen-year-old immigrant brain couldn't process it. I knew I was Filipino; that much was clear. But I didn't realize I was "Asian," or that Chinese and Korean and Indian people were "Asian," too, and that because I was Filipino, I was both "Asian" and a "Pacific Islander." Calling people "Hispanic" or "Latino" was perplexing to me, partly due to the fact that people assumed I was Hispanic or Latino because of my name. (My stock answer: "The Philippines was colonized by the Spanish, who gave us their Spanish names.") Are people labeled "Asian" for geographic reasons, because we came from the "Asian" continent? But, if it was about geography, shouldn't "Hispanic" and "Latino" people be called "Americans"? According to the maps—and to the Miss Universe pageants that I religiously watched as a kid—"Hispanic" and "Latino" people were from Central and South America. What was the difference among these Americas? People come from the Philippines, from Mexico, from Egypt, from France. As far as I could tell, "white" was not a country. Neither was "black." I looked at the maps. Are people "Asian" and "Hispanic" because Americans started labeling people "black" and "white"? Did America make all of this up? And whenever I read anything about race, why are "Asian" and "Hispanic" capitalized while "black" and "white" are not? Where do you go if you are multiracial and multiethnic?

"You're such an FOB," my classmate Kristine told me during lunch as I ate rice and fish.

FOB, I would later learn, meant "fresh off the boat." It took me a while to realize that people like Kristine, who were born in the U.S. but whose parents come from the Philippines, are Filipino American. People like me, the ones who are new to America, are called FOBs. I didn't know where an FOB fit in the Asian/Pacific Islander/Hispanic dynamic.

I'll never forget the day of the O. J. Simpson verdict. I had no idea who Simpson was. But most of my classmates seemed to know, and most everyone had an opinion on what he did and why he did it, including my teachers, all of whom were white. On the day of the verdict, Mrs. Wakefield, who taught social studies, stopped the class and turned on the radio so everyone could listen. When Simpson was acquitted, the school erupted, the reaction spilling from the classrooms into the quad. It was the first time I saw race physically divide people. Black students cheered the outcome, white students jeered it, and Latino and Asian students—who made up more than half the school—looked at each other, wondering which side to join. This dynamic—Latinos and Asians seemingly left out of the black-and-white binary—would become a dominant question in my life. Where do I go? Do I go black? Do I go white? Can I do both?

"You're not black, you're not white," Mrs. Wakefield told me during one of our afternoon chats. An elderly white woman, she walked around campus with chalk all over her hair, with oversize eyes that could see more than what you were willing to share. Mrs. Wakefield was the first teacher I developed a friendship with.

"Consider yourself lucky."

I didn't. I was just mystified. But what was becoming clear—and what I started internalizing during my years at Crittenden—was that race was a tangible, torturous, black-or-white thing in a country where conversations about how you identify and whom you represent largely fall into two extremes. Nonblack, nonwhite people had to figure out which side they fell on and to which degree.

In my early formative days in America, while observing my classmates and watching TV and movies, I learned that race was as much about behavior—perceived behavior, expected behavior—as it was about physicality. "Don't be too white," I overheard my Mexican classmates tell each other. "Why are you acting so black?" my Filipino friends said to one another. None of the comments sounded complimentary. Sometimes the comments from my nonwhite, nonblack classmates were as negative toward "white" people as they were toward "black" people. Too often I stayed silent because I didn't know what to say.

I wasn't sure how a Filipino was supposed to look, or where a Filipino was supposed to fit.

5

FILIPINOS

Filipinos fit everywhere and nowhere at all.

We are the invisible of the invisibles, a staggering feat considering that the worldwide Filipino population stands at 115 million: about 105 million live in the Philippine islands (making the Philippines the world's twelfth-most-populous country, just below Mexico); and an additional ten million are scattered across a hundred countries, most of whom are permanent legal residents or citizens of one of those countries. Of the ten million overseas Filipinos, more than 3.5 million live in the U.S., making us the second-largest

Asian group in the U.S. Even though one out of five Asian Americans is Filipino, many of us don't identify as Asian. Our Filipinotowns aren't as visible as Koreatowns and Chinatowns. Wherever we are and however we self-identify, non-Filipinos have an interesting way of identifying us. Even though our jobs are as varied as our people—we're nurses and lawyers, artists and professors—most people I meet seem to think of us as servants. Apparently, we are among the most sought-after group of domestic workers. I've lost count of how many times someone told me, out of the blue, "You guys make the best nannies and maids."

Perhaps that's because Filipino culture, while proud of its singularity and eccentricity, is so malleable. Adaptability was essential for surviving 420 years of emotional and physical ravages.

The Philippine islands were "discovered" by Spanish colonialists who ruled them for more than 370 years until the Americans, desperate to expand their economic and political reach, craved empire. The United States declared itself the rightful "owner" of the islands for some fifty years. My birth country's colonial history consists of being "300 years in the convent" and "50 years in Hollywood." My grandparents embodied this unshakable colonial-imperial reality. Both devout Catholics—the Philippines is the only predominantly Catholic country in Asia—Lolo learned English words and phrases by listening to Frank Sinatra and Dean Martin in jukeboxes, while Lola preferred Nat King Cole and Ella Fitzgerald.

Some of my Filipino American friends joke that Americans only remember Filipinos when they need us to house their naval fleet and fight their battles. Consider the fate of Filipino soldiers who fought the Japanese during World War II. With the promise of U.S. citizenship and full veteran benefits, more than 250,000 Filipino soldiers fought under the American flag, playing a crucial role in achieving victory. Shortly after, the Rescission Act of 1946 retroactively took away these soldiers' status as U.S. veterans. The message was clear: Your service didn't matter. It took more than sixty years to rectify the injustice.

From the outset, this dynamic has been complicated by race and skin color. During the Philippine-American War, white American soldiers in the Philippines referred to Filipinos as "niggers" because of their dark complexion. When Filipinos first arrived in California, in the early to mid-1900s, confused Americans placed them in the same ethnic category as Mongolians. In California, local authorities imposed laws on Filipinos prohibiting them from marrying Caucasians, and Filipinos had to drive out of state in order to marry white women. Throughout the Great Depression, white Americans claimed that Filipinos "brought down the standard of living because they worked for low wages." Many hotels, restaurants, and even swimming pools displayed signs that read "POSITIVELY NO FILIPINOS ALLOWED!"

In spite of all of this, America was still a "promised land" for Filipinos eager to escape poverty and provide for their families. After all, if Americans could come and claim the Philippines, why couldn't Filipinos move to America?

With the colonial conquest of the Philippines came a real awareness, and division, based on skin color. I was born to parents who were considered the *mestizos* (light-skinned ones) in their own families. I am the only child of Emelie Salinas and Jose Lito Vargas. Shortly after they got married, it became apparent that they had been too young to wed, much less have a child. From the start, their parents had to help them financially. My father was one of nine children; his mother, Dolores, was the second wife of Ramon, a businessman in the capital city of Manila. I don't remember ever meeting Ramon. My mother was the only daughter of Teofilo and Leonila, a lower-middle-class couple in Iba, a rural *barangay* (town) in Zambales, an agricultural province dotted with unlimited rice farms and the sweetest heart-shaped mangoes you'll ever taste. To this day, when I see mangoes at grocery stores I am reminded of Iba. All over Zambales were beautiful rivers with crystalline waters where we bathed and washed our laundry. Teofilo was a high school dropout; Leonila did not make it past sixth grade. My parents separated before I learned to speak, and, if family lore is to be believed, the first words I ever spoke were "Lolo" and "Lola." As the first *apo* (grandchild) of Teofilo and Leonila, I was treasured, treated as if I were their own child.

If you lived in Zambales at the time, there were three primary ways to get to America: (1) join the U.S. Navy; (2) marry a U.S. citizen; (3) get petitioned by a relative. Lolo's younger sister, Florie, fell in love with an American who served in the U.S. Marines. They married, and Florie headed to America in 1963, becoming a U.S. citizen by 1966. When Florie asked Lolo if he wanted to come to America and bring his family, Lolo did not hesitate. Across the developing country, which was mired in political corruption, people believed that going to America was the golden ticket to better jobs, better wages, a better life. Because of the 1965 Immigration and Nationality Act that ended decades-long racial and ethnic quotas and favored family unification, Florie was able to file a petition to bring Lolo to the United States. The wait took almost two decades. In 1984, when I was three years old, Lolo and Lola left Zambales for California.

The only things I've ever gotten from my father were his name and his thick eyebrows. By the time Lolo and Lola left, Papa had abandoned Mama and me. For as long as I can remember, Mama and her parents cared for me. Since she was the daughter in the family, who was expected to marry and have kids, Lolo told Mama to drop out of school so her younger brother could go to college. (Lolo could only afford to send one kid to school.) Mama left me in the care of relatives as she looked for odd jobs, which were hard to find for a woman with no college degree. After a while, Lolo and Lola told Mama to stop trying to find work and focus on raising me. They began supporting us. The Philippines is one of the world's largest recipients of remittances; Lolo and Lola were among the estimated 3.5 million Filipinos in the U.S. who would send monthly checks to relatives that the Philippine economy could not survive without, creating a culture of consumerism and a cycle of financial dependency that I was part of before I even knew who I was.

As a toddler in Iba, before Lolo and Lola emigrated to America, I grew up in a house made of cement and wood with a makeshift bathroom. Running water was precious in the provinces, and we cleaned ourselves, including bathing, using the *tabo* system. *Tabo* are vessels used to take water from a *timba* (pail). That way, water is not wasted. (Before the Americans took over, coconut shells served as *tabo*. Americans introduced Filipinos to plastic, and plastic *tabo* were born.) Once Lolo and Lola moved to the U.S., Mama and I moved to Pasig, in the capital city, living in a rented apartment with running water—paid for, of course, by Lolo and Lola.

Growing up in Pasig, I thought of Lolo and Lola as wealthy people who had unlimited American dollars and an endless supply of M&M's candy and cans and cans of Spam, which they regularly shipped to us in what is called a *balikbayan* (repatriate) box—an eighteen-by-twenty-four-inch box that came to the Philippines at least four times every year, containing all the American goods that my grandparents wanted to send us. It was not until I arrived in California to live with them that I discovered that they were not rich. In fact, they barely survived, working low-paying jobs: she as a food server, he as a security guard. To this day, I don't know how they managed to stretch every earned dollar. They didn't own a sprawling home, as I had imagined, but rented a modest three-bedroom house from Lolo's sister Florie. One of the bedrooms was for Lolo and Lola; one bedroom I shared with Uncle Rolan, my mother's younger brother; and the third bedroom they rented out to a friend. Lolo usually worked the overnight shift, while Lola and Uncle Rolan worked during the day. After school, I was in charge of raking the leaves from the lawn, taking out the trash, and making sure the dishes were always washed. If I'd been an obedient son in Pasig, I was an even more obedient grandson in Mountain View. In my mind, it was all I could do to help Lolo and Lola as they struggled to make ends meet, paying all their monthly bills while continuing to support my mama with a monthly allowance. Uncle Rolan, who worked in accounting, paid for whatever expenses I needed at school. At this point, Mama had a steady boyfriend named Jimmy, who worked overseas from time to time. Their daughter, Czarina, my half sister, was barely two years old when I left. Two years after I came to America, they had a son, Carl, my half brother, whom I haven't met. Jimmy helped raise them and continues to provide support.

Even though Lolo and Lola arrived in the U.S. nearly a decade before I did, I was their introduction to America. It's not unusual in immigrant families for the younger kids to be the ones who help parents and grandparents understand their adopted culture. Our home was decidedly Filipino. Lola could tell you the news from Manila, but would struggle to explain what was happening in San Francisco, just an hour north of us. We spoke either Tagalog or Sambali, the dialects spoken by the people of Zambales. We ate only Filipino food, mostly rice, fish, and pork. We mostly interacted with Filipino friends and relatives. We used the *tabo* system even though we had running water.

Google was founded less than two miles from our house, which is not too far from Stanford University. Mountain View is near the geographic heart of Silicon Valley, the storied region in the San Francisco Bay Area that runs on engineers and entrepreneurs placing their bets as they search for the next new thing. I grew up in the poorer part of Mountain View in the 1990s, before Apple, in nearby Cupertino, was dubbed "the most valuable brand in the world," and before Facebook, in nearby Menlo Park, would revolutionize the social media era. These days, the Bay Area is home to the third highest number of billionaires in the world. Millionaires abound. Renting an apartment can cost upward of three thousand dollars a month, and you'd be hard-pressed to buy a home for less than a million dollars. On any given day, at any given time, you'll spot a few Teslas on the road.

But my family is from the *other* Mountain View, which is part of the *other* Silicon Valley. This is the Mountain View of immigrant families who live in cramped houses and apartments, who depend on Univision, Saigon TV News, and the Filipino Channel for news of home, not the homes they're living in but the homes they left behind. This is the Silicon Valley of ethnic grocery stores in nondescript and dilapidated buildings, where sacks of rice and pounds of pork are cheaper, where you hear some Spanish, Tagalog, and Vietnamese before you hear a word of English. This is the *other* Mountain View, in the *other* Silicon Valley, where the American Dream rests on the outdated and convoluted immigration system that requires families to wait for years, if not decades, to be reunited with their loved ones.

Where I grew up, Filipinos who populated public schools struggled to figure out where we belonged in an America that sees itself as mostly black and white. If America is a wobbly three-legged stool, with white Americans and black Americans each taking a leg, the third leg is divided between Latinos and Asians, whose histories of struggle and oppression are often maligned and neglected. I'm not sure which leg Native Americans would stand on. As for the Filipinos, we are stuck in the middle of one leg of that wobbly stool.

6

MEXICAN JOSÉ AND FILIPINO JOSE

"Where's your green card?" Mexican José was asking me.

We were sitting in the very back of the room. It was seventh-period science class, and Mr. Album was doing his best to keep everyone awake.

"Huh?" I snapped back, totally confused. "What?"

In my classes at Crittenden, there were only two Joses: Mexican José and Filipino Jose. Me.

"Your green card," Mexican José said, before pulling a plastic-covered card from his back pocket. "It's the card you need to bring with you to school. You know, if you're an immigrant."

I remembered the short television ads I'd been seeing at home, playing over and over again. The ads were about Proposition 187, a ballot initiative that sought to ban "illegal" people from using public services. When people voted in the next election, they could also vote yes or no on enacting a new law, called Proposition 187. The 1994 race for California governor was engulfed by Proposition 187. The Republican incumbent, Pete Wilson, was arguing that it was unfair for Americans to support "illegal immigrant children" attending American schools, costing taxpayers $1.5 billion a year. I remembered being confused by the ad. I didn't know who "illegal immigrant children" were and couldn't conceive of what $1.5 billion represented. Wilson said that his opponent, a Democrat named Kathleen Brown, would rather spend money on "illegals" than take care of "California's children." The ad ended by asking: "Where do you stand?"

Whenever "illegals" were brought up in the news, either on television or in the newspapers and magazines I scoured at the library, the focus was on Latinos and Hispanics, specifically Mexicans. It wasn't about Lolo and Lola, or Uncle Rolan and Uncle Conrad, or Lolo's younger sisters, Florie and Rosie. It wasn't about me. I didn't know that the immigration law that allowed my Filipino family to legally come here is the very same law that created "illegal immigration" as we know it. While the 1965 Immigration and Nationality Act benefited Asian immigrants, it put Latinos at a disadvantage. Before 1965, immigration from Mexico and other Latin

American countries was largely unrestricted. There was a government guest worker system called the bracero program that permitted millions of Mexican nationals to work in the U.S. to fill World War II farm-labor shortages. Two separate events—the dissolution of the bracero program and the enactment of the 1965 immigration law—created an "illegal immigrant" problem where there had been none. When the bracero program ended, many former bracero workers continued crossing the border to fill the same jobs, but now illegally. The combination of the end of the bracero program and limits on legal immigration from the Western Hemisphere fueled the rise of illegal immigration.

I knew none of this as Mexican José showed me his green card.

All I knew was, I was not Mexican.

"I guess you don't have to worry about your green card," Mexican José told me a couple of minutes later. "Your name is Jose, but you look Asian."

7

FAKE

The next time I thought about my green card, I was riding my mountain bike to the nearby Department of Motor Vehicles office, just across the street from Target.

Without telling anyone in the family, I decided I was going to apply for a driver's permit. I was sixteen, the age when American teenagers were supposed to get their licenses. Sometimes, Lolo drove me to school but couldn't pick me up, so I often took the bus or bummed rides from friends. After Lolo bought me a newly painted black bike at a garage sale for fifty dollars, it was my primary way of getting around.

According to a DMV instruction booklet I had found at

the library, I had to bring proof of identification with me. Since I was an immigrant, that meant bringing my green card, which Lolo kept in a folder in a filing cabinet in his bedroom. With my green card and a school identification card tucked inside my geometry textbook, I filled out the application form, took my seat, and waited for my name to be called.

A few minutes later, I handed a curly-haired, bespectacled woman my school ID and green card. Without even looking at the school ID, she examined the green card, flipping it around, twice. Furrowing her brows, she then lowered her head, leaned over, and whispered, "This is fake. Don't come back here again."

Fake.

Instantly, I thought she was mistaken, perhaps even lying. She seemed surprised that I didn't know that the green card was fake. In fact, I was so sure that she was mistaken or lying that I didn't even bother to question her. I just assumed she was wrong, turned around, got on my bike, and pedaled home, accompanied by a mix tape of rock music and R & B, the music and lyrics muddling my thoughts.

Of course she's lying.

How can it be fake?

As I approached Mi Pueblo, a Mexican market where Lola and I sometimes shopped for mangoes and rice, my heart stopped.

Maybe the woman at the DMV thought I was Mexican? Because, you know, my name is Jose even though it's not José?

I returned home, my confusion starting to turn into a full-fledged panic attack. But I was sure everything would be fine. Lolo would clear everything up as he always did. Lolo had always taken care of everyone in the family. He stood no more than five foot seven inches tall but loomed over everyone, speaking in a clipped, overenunciated English that exuded clarity. Since Lolo worked the graveyard shift, he was often home in the afternoon. He was hunched over a table in the garage, cutting grocery coupons from newspapers, a cigarette dangling from his lips, when I arrived. I dropped my bike on the ground, searched for the green card in my backpack, and ran toward him.

"Peke ba ito?" I asked in Tagalog. ("Is this fake?") I held out the green card and searched his face as my voice cracked, afraid of what he might say.

Without addressing the question, he got up, swiped the card from my hand, and uttered a sentence that changed the course of my life.

"Huwag mong ipakita yang sa mga tao." ("Don't show it to people.")

His voice was soft, soaking in shame.

"Hindi ka dapat nandito." ("You are not supposed to be here.")

The shock of hearing that sentence, spoken by the very

man who had sacrificed so much to bring his first grandson to America, still haunts me. Nothing Lolo ever said to me afterward—nothing Lola or Mama has said to me since—weighed as heavily.

I was speechless. In English and Tagalog. I don't remember what I said. But so many questions came darting from all directions that I thought my head would burst open to make room for them.

If this green card is "fake," then what else is "fake"?

Who else knows that this card is "fake"? Lola? Uncle Rolan? Does Mama know? Why didn't anybody tell me?

Can I get a "real" green card?

Is a "real" green card something you can buy?

For how much?

Where?

Can I tell my friends about this?

Can I trust my family?

Who can I trust?

All I knew was that I could barely trust myself—what I was feeling and how I was dealing with the shock. It was disorienting, as though gravity had changed and I could float away. Nothing was as it seemed. No one was who I thought they were, least of all myself. I was confused. I was angry. Angry at myself for having gone to the DMV to begin with. Angry at Lolo for putting me in this position, which I did not create. Angry at Mama. They conspired to send me to

America to give me a better life without realizing they had created a nightmare scenario for me.

And I was scared.

Above all, it was the hardening—the emotional hardening—that I remembered most from that afternoon and the subsequent days and weeks.

Something within me hardened, and it became a place no one else could go. That I would not allow anyone else to broach. I felt betrayed in ways I couldn't yet articulate to myself or fully face.

My first instinct was to run. But there was nowhere to go, no one else to stay with. Another idea I had was to fly back to the Philippines, to go home to Mama. But Lolo told me that even the passport I used to get to America was fake. The photo in that passport was mine, but the name was not. He then told me that he'd bought me another passport with my name on it but not my *complete* name. Instead of Jose Antonio Salinas Vargas, he put my name as Jose Antonio Abaga Vargas. Salinas was Lolo's last name, the middle name that I have on my birth certificate. Abaga was Lola's maiden name. In case we got caught in a lie, he did not want his name, the Salinas name, involved. Salinas is the maiden name of Florie, his beloved sister, and the reason Lolo and Lola were able to emigrate in the first place. Salinas is the last name of Conrad, his favorite nephew. Neither Lola, Florie, nor Uncle Conrad knew of Lolo's scheme. Together, the fake green card and the passports cost Lolo forty-five hundred dollars, a huge sum for a security guard who made five dollars an hour.

It took me time to make sense of the gravity of the deception, the layers of lies. I couldn't stay legally. I couldn't leave legally, either. I was trapped. A legal no-boy's-land.

Later that night, on a phone call with Mama, I demanded answers to questions I had never imagined I would have to ask. I found out that the "uncle" who accompanied me on the flight to America was a smuggler whom Lolo had paid. The morning I left the Philippines was so rushed because Mama hadn't known when I would be leaving. The smuggler didn't give an exact date or time. The plan was that the smuggler would call hours before my flight was set to depart. I had to be ready at all times. Unbeknownst to me, my suitcase had been packed for months.

They had to lie about me because they lied about everything else.

After Lolo arrived in America, he petitioned for his two children to follow: Mama and Uncle Rolan. But instead of listing Mama as a married woman, which she still was, at least in the eyes of the law, Lolo lied and listed her as single. As a legal resident, which he was at the time, he could not petition for his married children. Even more important, Lolo didn't care for my father, who had abandoned Mama and me; he didn't want my father to come here. Lolo lied on the petition.

The lie scared Lolo. He grew nervous that immigration

officials would discover that Mama was married, jeopardizing not only her chances of coming here but also those of Uncle Rolan. Lolo withdrew Mama's petition. After Uncle Rolan legally came to America in 1991, Lolo tried to get my mother here through a tourist visa. But her application was denied three times. Mama was unemployed; she couldn't prove that she wouldn't just overstay her visa and illegally remain in America, because she had nothing substantial to come back to. So, at Lolo's urging, she decided to send me to America with a smuggler. She figured she would find some way to follow me soon, within months, maybe a year at most, as she had promised that morning at the airport. But she couldn't find a way.

Their plan was to buy time until I could become legal. Lolo expected me to work under-the-table jobs. Maybe at the flea market where his older brother, David, and his wife, Modesta—Uncle Conrad's parents—cleaned bathrooms. *"Maganda ang trabaho iyan,"* Lolo said. ("It's a decent job.") Or maybe as a cashier at Fry's Electronics, where one of his friends was a supervisor. Once I had a job, Lola said I would find a woman who was a U.S. citizen to marry. That was the way to "get legal" and become a "citizen." I would save up money to pay the woman. Maybe I wouldn't even need to pay her, because I might even fall in love with her.

"Hindi ko gagawin niyan," I told Mama on the phone. ("I'm not doing it.")

"Hindi ako magpapakasal." (I'm not getting married.")

Shortly after that unforgettable day, I would learn that in Filipino culture, there's a term for someone who is in America illegally: "TNT," short for *tago ng tago*, which translates to "hiding and hiding." Finding out I was a TNT was not only the beginning of the lies I had to tell and what I had to do to "pass" as "American," but the beginning of the way I hid myself from Lolo, Lola, and Mama.

8

PLAYING A ROLE

I swallowed American culture before I learned how to chew it.

Being an American felt like a role I had to portray, in an improvised one-man play I made up after I found out I was not supposed to be in America.

Talk like an American.

Write like an American.

Think like an American.

Pass as an American.

I was the sixteen-year-old actor, producer, and director of

this production, inhabiting a character that I honed with the help of a fourteen-inch TV set, a VCR, an audio player that played cassettes and CDs, and library cards from both the Mountain View Public Library and the Los Altos Library. Though there were libraries in the Philippines, I don't recall going into one while I was growing up. Here in America, the libraries were my church, and I was an acolyte. Between the two libraries—one with an extensive collection of videos of American films, the other boasting every CD you'd ever want to listen to—my education was complete. Lolo had bought the secondhand TV set at a garage sale for thirty-five dollars when I moved to America. As a sixteenth birthday gift, Lolo and Lola bought me the brand-new VCR that could record TV shows.

What I watched on TV led to what movies I looked for, what music I listened to, what books, magazines, and newspapers I read. There is no such thing as winter in the Philippines—no ice, no snow—so I was instantly drawn to figure skating. I couldn't believe people were spinning and jumping on a quarter-inch of a blade. The saga of Nancy Kerrigan and Tonya Harding made competitive skating more popular; there was a competition every weekend. Before skaters began their "programs," the titles of the music they skated to were flashed on TV. Skating was my introduction to Rachmaninoff, Beethoven, Mozart, et al. Did you know there are two versions of *Romeo and Juliet*, the Tchaikovsky version and the Prokofiev version? I borrowed all of it from the library. It was free. I couldn't believe it was free. Listening to rap and hip-hop while trying to understand Alanis Morissette and Joni Mitchell was my passport to black *and* white America; I thought that if I was fluent in both cultures, speaking in both tongues, no one would ask where I was from and how I got here. (It took me a while to discover that Alanis and Joni were both Canadians.) The 1990s was the beginning of hip-hop's rise as the most popular genre of music, particularly among young people. I convinced myself that reciting the lyrics to every one of Lauryn Hill's and Tupac Shakur's songs was proof of my American-ness. When I heard about a thing called country music, and couldn't find that much country music at the libraries, I went to Tower Records and listened to songs by Garth Brooks and Dolly Parton.

For me, movies were like a field trip, a way of seeing just how vast the country is. I didn't just watch all the animated Disney films, from *The Little Mermaid* to *Beauty and the Beast* and *Aladdin*. In a span of a few weeks, I watched *Goodfellas, Do the Right Thing,* and *Working Girl.* I was floored when I realized that they were all filmed in a place called New York City. How can Martin Scorsese's New York City be the same as Spike Lee's New York City and Mike Nichols's New York City? That was my introduction to perspective. After watching *Sophie's Choice, Silkwood, Out of Africa,* and *A Cry in the Dark,* I went up to a librarian and asked: "Is there more than one Meryl Streep?"

Watching TV was a different kind of cultural immersion. *TV Guide*, a weekly magazine that I bought at the grocery store, was a bible. TV is where I picked up idioms and mannerisms. I learned how to use "cool beans" from *Full House*. In order to act, talk, and pass as some kind of American, I studied every show I could watch, from *Frasier* and *The Fresh Prince of Bel-Air* to *The West Wing*. Imitating how Bill Moyers spoke on PBS while listening to Tupac in my CD player seemed as far away from the "illegal" Filipino with a thick accent as I could get.

Airing on weekday afternoons, *The Oprah Winfrey Show* unlocked doors in my imagination. Oprah's show introduced me to authors like Maya Angelou, Wally Lamb, and Toni Morrison—oh, how Oprah loved Morrison, whose books she often selected for her book club. I was drawn to Angelou because she bore a resemblance to Lola, with the same low and rich timbre of a voice. Watching TV introduced me to Broadway, including the actress and singer Audra McDonald, whose voice was so expansive—swinging and soaring, walloping and wailing—it seemed to jump out of the screen and into my bedroom.

I didn't know what Broadway was, or how the Tony Awards differed from the Oscars or the Emmys, but because of McDonald, I recorded the 1998 Tony Awards on TV. About twenty minutes into the show, just as I was figuring out the difference between "Best Revival of a Play" and "Best New Play," a musical called *Ragtime* was introduced.

Over a simple melody, a young boy took center stage, later to be joined by his father and mother and other white people from a place called New Rochelle, New York.

A beat later, the music changed to a syncopated tune, and a group of black people danced center stage. A black man sitting in front of a piano took over. He declared: *"Up in Harlem, people danced to a music that was theirs and no one else's. The sound of changing time. The music of a better day."*

Yet again the music changed, signaling the arrival of something mysterious as a new group of people— immigrants—took center stage. A bearded man with some kind of accent (I couldn't place where it was from) said:

> *They came from Western and Eastern Europe by the thousands.*
> *No dream was too big.*
> *They would be the next J. P. Morgan, Evelyn Nesbit, or Henry Ford. It would be their century, too. It was only 1906.*

My mind raced as the white people, the black people, and the immigrants crowded the stage. At this point, members of the three groups started spreading out, then began to self-segregate, before finally moving into separate areas of the stage while the music's melody turned dissonant and discordant.

I watched this performance so many times that I wore out the tape. The "immigrants" in the performance didn't look like Mexicans or Filipinos or Chinese or Indians or Pakistanis—what people usually think of when they hear "immigrants." It wasn't until watching that performance that I realized that white people were immigrants, too, that they came from somewhere: Ireland, Germany, Italy, Latvia, Russia, etc. Obsessing over *Ragtime* led to discovering the works of Oscar Hammerstein, Richard Rodgers, Irving Berlin, George Gershwin, and Stephen Sondheim, all of whom, I would realize, came from immigrant backgrounds. *Ragtime* connected dots I didn't know existed, allowing me to better understand American history in ways my textbooks didn't fully explain. I would learn that except for Native Americans, whose tribes were already here before the colonists and the Pilgrims landed, and African Americans, who were uprooted from their homes and imported to this country as slaves, everyone was an immigrant. I didn't know what legal papers they had, or if they needed them, or if they were considered "illegals" too, but white people were immigrants, like my family are immigrants. After doing some research at the libraries, I discovered that *Ragtime* was based on a historical novel by E. L. Doctorow, whose book told the changing story of America through real-life personalities and fictionalized characters at the turn of the twentieth century. Each time I watched the tape, every time I listened to the song, I wondered where Latinos, Asians, Africans, Caribbeans, Middle Easterners—the new immigrants of the past few decades—fit on that stage and in the evolving American story. I wondered where my Mexican friends fit. I wondered where Lolo, Lola, and I fit, if we fit at all.

We spoke Taglish at home—a combination of the Tagalog that Lolo and Lola spoke, and the answers I gave in English. Except for the 11:00 p.m. local news, Lolo and Lola watched only the Filipino Channel, a cable network that re-aired shows from the Philippines. Sometimes, I watched the shows with everyone. More often than not, though, I was in my room.

The only time I saw a Hollywood movie starring people who looked anything like my family was *The Joy Luck Club*, which, I learned later on, was based on a book by a Chinese American writer, Amy Tan. I picked up the movie at the video store, drawn to the VHS cover: the smiling faces of four Asian women and a striking shot of the Golden Gate Bridge. I rented the tape and watched it late one night in the living room when everyone was sleeping.

We shared one bathroom. After Lola used the bathroom that night, she saw me in the living room. She sat down on the opposite side of the couch. We said nothing to each other. *The Joy Luck Club* was the first American film Lola and I watched together. I'm not sure how much she understood the interlocking stories of four Chinese women who emigrated to America in search of better lives. But she understood it enough that she started to cry when one of the characters, Lindo, broke into tears as she explained her love for her American-born daughter, Waverly. I ended up watching Lola watch the movie, wondering how much she had given up to come here, how rarely she got to see her own daughter. At that moment, I realized it wasn't just me who missed my mother—Lola longed for my mama, too. But I was too selfish to want to see it, too absorbed with my own pain.

I couldn't tell my family that I did not want to marry a woman to "get legal" and become a "citizen" because I am gay.

There's nothing wrong with being gay.

I don't know exactly how many times I must have said it to myself, like some kind of personal anthem, in the subsequent months. *There's nothing wrong with being gay.* I said it enough times to myself that, on May 27, 1999, I ended up blurting it out loud as I sat in the back of room 102 during U.S. history class.

Some of my classmates turned around. A student named Anna started to cry. She told the class about her gay uncle. Even though I felt how uncomfortable some people were, I remember feeling quite comfortable, as if I had opened a window and let some light into what was a very dark room—the room inside my head.

With that announcement, I became the only openly gay student at Mountain View High School.

Lying about my immigration status was one lie too many. I didn't want to lie about being gay. Coming out as gay allowed me to exert control over a life I had no control over. It was not my decision to come here, acquire fake papers, and lie my way into being in America. But I was here. At the very least, I felt that I had to control what kind of American I was going to be, what kind of cultural connections I was going to make, which led to what kind of mask I had to wear.

9

MOUNTAIN VIEW HIGH SCHOOL

The moment I realized that writing for newspapers meant having a "byline"—"by Jose Antonio Vargas," my name in print, on a piece of paper, visible and tangible—I was hooked.

There are no writers in my family—not on my mother's side, not on my father's side. In the Philippines, we're a family of farmers, nurses, cooks, accountants, construction workers, U.S. Navy veterans. I got into journalism because of a high school teacher.

"You ask too many annoying questions," Mrs. Dewar told me.

Mrs. Dewar taught English composition to high school sophomores like me. Mrs. Dewar was also the longtime adviser to the *Oracle*, the student newspaper. She had wanted to be a journalist herself, and she told me of a free, two-week journalism camp for "minority" journalists at San Francisco State University, her alma mater. When I asked her what a journalist does, she quipped, "It's for annoying people like you who love to ask questions."

What drew me to journalism? First, it was a sign of rebellion and independence from my family, a way of rejecting Lolo's strategy of working under-the-table jobs until I married a woman and got my papers.

Second, and more importantly, writing was a form of existing, existing through the people I interviewed and the words I wrote as I struggled with where I fit in. Writing was also a way of belonging, a way of contributing to society. Being a journalist is a public service, the opposite of the stereotype that "illegals" have come to the U.S. to take, take, take. It didn't occur to me initially, but the more stories I reported on, the more people I interviewed, the more I realized that writing was the freest thing I could do. It wasn't limited by borders and legal documents, but largely dependent on my skills and talent. Reporting, interviewing, and writing felt like the safest, surest place in my everyday reality. If I was not considered an American because I didn't have the right papers, then practicing journalism—writing in English, interviewing Americans, making sense of the people and places around me—was my way of writing myself into America. In the beginning, writing was only a way of passing as an American. I never expected it to be an identity. Above all else, I write to exist, to make myself visible.

Instantly, journalism became not just a passion but *the* driving force in my life. Everything, and everyone, took a back seat to my work. Getting good grades at school took a back seat to my being a reporter. If it didn't have anything to do with furthering my career in journalism, I didn't do it. After returning from the "minority" summer camp of mostly Latino and black high school students, I called the *Mountain View Voice*, my local weekly community newspaper, and talked my way into an unpaid internship. I was desperate to get this internship. For a few weeks, all the job entailed was answering the phones and buying coffee for the top editor, an overworked man named Rufus Jeffris. But when a fire erupted three blocks from where I lived and there were no other reporters to cover it, the editor sent me. My first-ever front-page story was about a fire on Farley Street, where I grew up.

"Blackened scraps of clothing carefully piled on a corner of the front lawn were the only items that Mitch and Linda Radisich were able to salvage from their home at 1151 Farley Street after a fire gutted the residence on June 16," read the "lede" (the opening sentence) of the news story, which took up a third of the entire front page. I was proud of that lede, especially of the verbs "salvage" and "gutted." News writing, especially breaking news writing, I learned early on, depended on verbs. It was all about action.

"Anong ginagawa mo?" ("What are you doing?") Lolo exclaimed when he saw my byline on the front page of the *Voice.*

"Bakit nasa diyaryo ang pangalan mo?" ("Why is your name in the newspaper?")

The angrier Lolo became, the more independent I felt. I didn't need his approval. Even if I did, he couldn't give it. Lolo had to ask me what "blackened" meant.

"Masyado ka nang nagiging sosyal," Lolo said. "You're getting fancy now."

Fancy or not, I made a concerted effort to stay as busy as possible. The busier my schedule was, the more activities I committed to, the less time I had to spend at home. Being at home—seeing Lolo and Lola, realizing how much they worried for me—reminded me of my limitations. Being at school opened up possibilities. In addition to writing for both the *Voice* and *Oracle,* I sang in choir, competed in speech and debate tournaments, acted in and directed plays and musicals, and was elected by the student government to represent their interests to the school board. I was so omnipresent at school that teachers, administrators, and parents of my classmates took notice. I neglected to tell Lolo and Lola about parent-teacher nights and open houses at school.

I went alone and represented myself. It was easier that way.

"Don't you ever go home?" Pat Hyland, the school principal, asked me one night after speech and debate practice. Because I was probably the busiest student at school who did not drive, classmates and school staff gave me rides, including Pat. Pat was the earliest member of a bighearted community of strangers who, over time, would occupy essential roles in my life. Whenever she drove me home, we stopped and got some lattes at Starbucks on El Camino Real.

El Camino Real is the artery that runs through the peninsula south of San Francisco, dividing communities by race and class and separating adequate schools from great ones. Residents on its east side were generally on the lower end of the economic ring, mostly service workers and laborers. Folks on the west side, particularly the western parts of Mountain View and its neighboring towns, Los Altos and Los Altos Hills, were considerably more affluent, white-collar professionals and technology entrepreneurs who cashed in early and felt comfortable buying their kids convertible BMWs and Mercedes-Benzes. The parents of well-to-do students were generous to many other students from working-class families like mine, paying for field trips, no questions asked. Fees for speech competitions would be covered, with no trace of who paid for what. For the most part, you couldn't find anyone to thank because they didn't need or want thanking. If it sounds too benevolent to believe, just too good to be true, perhaps it was. Nevertheless, I was a product of this community. Sometimes I wonder what would have happened to me if I had attended a school where others couldn't afford to, or didn't care to, help those less fortunate.

Shortly after we met, Pat introduced me to Rich Fischer, her boss, the school district's superintendent. Though he was the highest-ranking official at the school, he didn't act like it. He was friendly and accessible, regularly roaming the school grounds interacting with both students and teachers. "Don't call me Mr. Fischer," he said during our first meeting. "It's Rich." Because I felt like I didn't fit in with my classmates, I was more comfortable with teachers and administrators.

I was elected as the student representative on the school board, which meant I ended up spending more time with Rich and his secretary, Mary; their relationship was less like boss and secretary than brother and sister. They were like a family unit, and they treated me like family. Over the years, Mary has written me more greeting cards—birthday cards, holiday cards, hope-you-feel-better cards—than anyone else I've ever met.

"There is always one moment in childhood," Graham Greene once wrote, "when the door opens and lets the future in." As the years passed, Pat, Rich, and Mary, among others, were the people who would find windows and try to open them when doors were shut. They did it because they could afford to; more importantly, they did it because they wanted to.

As I grew closer to Pat, Rich, and Mary, the distance

between Lolo, Lola, and me also grew. I saw less and less of them, because I spent more time at school and more time with my surrogate family. Pat, Rich, and Mary represented some kind of future for me. Lolo and Lola represented a past I was trying to run away from.

10

AN ADOPTED FAMILY

"What do you mean you're not applying to college?" Pat asked. While on our regular Starbucks stop, she was wondering why I hadn't shared anything about my college plans. This was the end of junior year, the time of fretting over college admission tests, the time of planning college tours.

I told Pat that I was not planning to go to college. I said I had a job lined up after high school, covering city hall and writing feature stories for the *Voice*, which would pay me between twenty-five and fifty dollars per article—a solid sum. I tried to sound proud of my plan, even though I felt defeated. College was never an option, especially after I found out that I was in the country illegally and that I couldn't apply for financial aid. But I couldn't tell Pat that. I had not told anyone except for Mrs. Denny, the choir teacher. Every spring the choir goes on tour. In the beginning of my junior year, Mrs. Denny announced to the class that we would be going to Japan. Shortly after, I pulled her to the corner of the room, near her desk, where no one could hear us.

"Mrs. Denny, I can't go to Japan."

"What do you mean?"

"I don't have the right papers."

"What are you talking about?"

She paused.

"We'll get you the right papers."

"No, no, you don't understand." I really didn't know what words to use, or if I could trust her with this information. All I could say was: "I don't have the right passport. I don't have the right green card."

Mrs. Denny's eyes parted like curtains. Her shoulders dropped. The only word she managed to say was, "Oh."

The following day, without giving me any warning, she told the whole class that the plan had changed. Instead of going to Japan, we would head to Hawaii. I don't remember if my classmates were disappointed or angry. What I will never get out of my mind was the reason that Mrs. Denny gave me when, years later, I asked her why she changed the plan: "I was not leaving any of my students behind."

All of the adults I knew at Mountain View High School wanted to make sure I wasn't left behind. Soon, everyone was asking about my college plans, including Gail Wade, the mother of one of my closest friends, Nathalie.

Without realizing it, I replaced Mama, to whom I barely spoke at the time, with Pat, Mary, and Gail. I couldn't talk to my own mother while I was collecting mother figures.

Eventually, I had to tell them the truth. I had no idea how they would react. I feared that they would reject me. One by one, I explained the fake green card, the fake passport, why I had to always bum rides to and from school, why college was not an option.

"Oh, now I understand why you don't drive," Rich said. "I couldn't figure out why."

This was in the early weeks of 2000, more than a year before legislation called the DREAM Act—short for the Development, Relief, and Education for Alien Minors Act, which would grant a path to legalization and citizenship for children brought to the U.S. illegally—would be introduced in Congress. At this point, there were no Dreamers and no one called anyone "undocumented." Teachers and educators, especially in more affluent communities like Mountain View, did not have much experience with the issue, much less know what to do with someone like me.

Pat and Rich spoke to lawyers separately; their families considered adopting me. But it was too late. Their lawyers said that because I was already over the age of sixteen, adoption wouldn't fix the problem. According to the lawyers, Lolo and Lola could have adopted me before I turned sixteen had they known it was an option. Although they were naturalized U.S. citizens, Lolo and Lola were wary of lawyers and fearful of the U.S. legal system.

At the time, I didn't know how to process this information. I was too numb to feel anger or heartbreak. I was so ashamed of myself, so ashamed of Lolo and Lola—of the situation that was created for me, a situation that I didn't know how to solve. I was too young to realize that the dream that Mama, Lolo, and Lola had for me was dictated by their own realities, by their own sense of limitations. The America they dreamed for me was not the America I was creating for myself.

If my adult mentors couldn't adopt me, they were determined to figure out a way to send me to college. They did, identifying a scholarship program that did not ask or care about my immigration status, established by a venture capitalist named Jim Strand, whose kids attended my school district. I received a four-year scholarship to college. I moved out of Lolo and Lola's house, and our separation seemed complete.

Soon after I got the scholarship, Jim and I met in person at a nearby coffee shop. He told me there were no criteria for the scholarship; he didn't care whether or not I had the right papers. The only thing that mattered was whether I really wanted to go to college and needed help. "Thank you very much," I said, and insisted on buying him his iced coffee. I had chosen to go to San Francisco State, which had hosted the summer camp that jump-started my journalism career. But that wasn't the only reason why. After finding out that my green card was fake—that the Alien Registration Number was not mine—I never wanted to be associated with a number. So, unlike most, if not all, of my college-bound classmates, I didn't take the SATs, the college admissions test. As it happened, San Francisco State didn't care about SAT scores so long as my grade point average was higher than 3.0. Since I already had a career, at least in my mind, I didn't really care much about grades or GPAs. Thankfully, mine ended up being higher than 3.0. It was 3.4.

As it turned out, I was the very first recipient of what is now called the MVLA Scholars. Jim donated one million dollars over five years to start the scholarship, and other parents and philanthropists have continued to fund it since. Since its inception eighteen years ago, more than 350 students have received support from the scholarship. According to the scholarship's administrators, all of whom are volunteers from the community, about 98 percent of the 137 students that they are currently supporting are the first in their family to attend college in America. Of those 137 students, 36 happen to be undocumented. Along with Jim, I now serve on the scholarship's advisory board.

11

BREAKING THE LAW

The first time I willfully broke the law, I was sitting in a small conference room on the third floor of the *San Francisco Chronicle* building.

It was spring 2000. I was just about to graduate from high school and was planning on moving to San Francisco for college. In the meantime, I got an entry-level job at the *Chronicle*. I'd answer the phone and deliver people's mail and faxes, but I could also pitch articles on the side. In was in.

That was how I found myself inside the *Chronicle* building filling out an employment form. Until that point, I had only been volunteering or doing contract jobs, nothing serious, certainly nothing that required legal paperwork. Since my discovery at the DMV, I avoided talking about paperwork, just as I avoided any conversation about driving. I had never filled out an employment form before.

The form asked for my full name, home address, date of birth, and phone number. That was the easy part.

Then came two dreaded statements, both in bold letters. The first:

> ❏ I am aware that federal law provides for imprisonment and/or fines for false statements or use of false documents in connection with the completion of this form.

The second:

> ❏ I attest, under penalty of perjury, that I am (check one of the following boxes):

They were followed by boxes, one of which I was supposed to check:

> ❏ A citizen or national of the United States
> ❏ A lawful permanent resident (Alien #) A
> ❏ An alien authorized to work until
> (Alien # or Admission #)

I am not a "lawful permanent resident." I am also not "an alien authorized to work." My "alien registration number," the number on the fake green card that Lolo bought me, belongs to someone else. I didn't know if that person was dead or alive; I didn't know what risk I would put that person in if I had used the number. I hated that I didn't know what I didn't know, and that I could potentially hurt someone. The only choice left was box number one, which was not really a choice because I am not a U.S. citizen. Not by birth. Not by law. Later, I would also learn that one of America's official laws states that it is "a criminal offense for anyone to falsely and willfully impersonate a citizen of the United States." Moreover, "whoever falsely and willfully represents himself to be a citizen of the United States shall be fined under this title or imprisoned not more than three years, or both."

But I wanted the job.

It meant independence, from Lolo and Lola, from Mama.

I needed the job.

Sweating under my brow, a couple of drops staining the form, I checked box number one.

Naïve as it sounds, I remember thinking: *Yes, I am lying. But I am going to earn this box.*

I don't remember how many times I said it to myself: *I am going to earn this box.*

What I always remember is hearing people say that people like me should "earn" our citizenship.

Exactly how I would earn being a citizen, I had no idea. What I did know, however, was that Lolo's lies were now my lies. I was no longer the blameless kid who wasn't aware of the circumstances of how I arrived in America. I was now a nineteen-year-old making a difficult and necessary choice to survive, which meant breaking the law.

What would you have done? Work under the table? Stay under the radar? Not work at all?

Which box would you check?

What have you done to earn your box?

Besides being born at a certain place in a certain time, did you have to do anything?

Anything at all?

If you wanted to get a job, if you wanted to have a life, if you wanted to exist as a human being, what would you have done?

12

AMBITION

The more ambitious as a reporter I became, the more risks I had to take, the more lies I had to tell, the more laws I had to break.

A few months after landing the entry-level job at the *Chronicle*, I applied for a paid summer internship at the *Philadelphia Daily News* in 2001. When the hiring recruiter asked if I had a driver's license and if I could drive, I lied and said yes to both. While working in Philadelphia, covering the police beat and writing breaking news stories, I took cabs and rode buses and the subway to get to my assignments.

A couple of times I had to hitchhike, making sure that no one found out. I couldn't tell the editors that I didn't have a license.

The 9/11 attacks changed immigration, legal and illegal, making it more difficult for people to come to America. In 2002, I applied for and was accepted to another paid summer internship, this time at the *Seattle Times*. Patricia Foote, the recruiter, emailed the summer interns to remind us to bring our proof of citizenship on our first day at work: a birth certificate, a passport, or a driver's license, plus an original Social Security card. I immediately called her. I took a leap of faith and told her about my immigration status. She sounded surprised and perplexed. And sympathetic—at least she sounded like it on the phone. She told me she had to consult a lawyer at the office and would get back to me. When she called, she withdrew the offer.

I didn't know this woman. She was a stranger, and now she knew my immigration status. I got paranoid. Paranoid enough that I decided to fly to Seattle. I'd never been to Seattle. I didn't know anyone who lived there. Using money that I saved up while working at the *Chronicle*, I booked my first-ever plane ticket, reserved my very first hotel room, and asked Patricia if we could meet in person. I don't remember exactly what we discussed while sitting across from each other at a diner, not too far from the *Times* office. But what I do remember was that I wanted to look her in the eye, to show that I was a real person, that I had a lot to lose if she told anyone else about my situation. I didn't ask her to keep my secret. Nevertheless, she didn't tell anyone about it.

Unfortunately, because I was honest about my immigration status, I lost the internship with the *Times*, even after I was accepted. I was crushed. Rich and Jim, whose scholarship sent me to college, suggested I meet with an immigration lawyer. Immigration is a complicated system, especially for undocumented people, and lawyers are needed to help navigate it. Jim covered the cost, and Rich accompanied me to the meeting in downtown San Francisco.

The meeting did not go well. The only solution for me, the lawyer said, was to leave the U.S., go back to the Philippines, and accept what's called a "10-year bar" before trying to come back to America, this time legally. The moment the lawyer said it, I was certain that it was the only solution. I hadn't seen Mama for almost ten years. Maybe it was time to go back, even if going back meant discarding what I'd done to build a life for myself here. I was so distraught at the thought of leaving that I didn't say a thing. In my mind, I was already starting to plan my trip back to Manila. I would stay there for the required ten years, and then try to come back to America.

As we walked down Montgomery Street, looking for his parked car, Rich broke the silence.

"You're not going anywhere. You're already here," Rich

said. "Put this problem on a shelf. Compartmentalize it. Keep going."

I'm not sure where my life would have gone without those words. Immediately, they altered my reality. Rich advised me to stay in the country and effectively break the law. Aside from leaving and going back to the Philippines, I didn't know what other options I had. Stay, and break the law. Leave, and perhaps never come back. So, when Rich said that I should put this problem on a shelf, that I should compartmentalize it, that I should keep going, it seemed like some kind of solution. *Put this problem on a shelf. Compartmentalize it. Keep going.*

So I did. The following summer, I applied for the internship program at eight newspapers, including the *Chicago Tribune*, the *Boston Globe*, and the *Washington Post*. To my surprise—and it *was* a surprise—I was accepted by all of them, including the *Post*. I didn't think I had much of a chance given how competitive it was. But I landed one of the twenty available spots. I got it! After Cheryl Butler, the recruiter, called to offer me the internship, I emailed myself notes from our conversation, just to make sure I had not imagined it.

Then the first person I called was Pat, my high school principal.

"Am I taking someone else's spot?" I asked. I always thought I was taking someone else's spot. After years of hearing that "illegals" were taking Americans' jobs, I was always worried that I didn't deserve to get chosen for a job.

She cackled.

"Don't be ridiculous," she said. "You earned it. Go."

But going meant needing a driver's license. Unlike in Philadelphia, where a license was not required, Cheryl, the recruiter, reminded me that I needed a license to get the job. I did not know how I would get around this requirement. What I did know was that I didn't want to lose an internship again, even if I had to lie to get it.

13

STRANGERS

Shortly after the holidays in 2003, I spent ten hours in the computer room at Mountain View's public library figuring out how to get a driver's license.

I googled every single state to find out its requirements. Each required a green card or a passport. Well, every state but Oregon. All Oregon required was a school ID, a birth certificate, and a proof of residency in Oregon. With the help of a friend whose father-in-law lived in Oregon, and with the help of my high school mentors, Pat, Rich, and Mary, I pretended to have an address in Oregon to get a driver's license so I could secure the internship.

In all those years I'd gotten closer to my second family, I never introduced Lolo to Pat, Rich, or Mary. Lolo disapproved of me going to the *Post*. Working in San Francisco was one thing; working in Washington, D.C., was a whole other thing. In Lolo's mind, I was risking too much.

"Hindi ka dapat nandito," Lolo would say. ("You are not supposed to be here.")

"Paano kung nahuli ka?" Lolo would ask. ("What if you get caught?")

I didn't answer Lolo. I walked away. That was always what I did whenever Lolo confronted me with the hard and cold truth of my situation. That I could get caught. That I was risking too much. That I was dreaming too big. Their fear for me burdened our relationship, so I saw less and less of them. A phone call here and there, a visit during Thanksgiving and Christmas, but that was it. I, too, feared getting caught, but I feared being stuck in one place even more.

I scored 71 on the driving test. A passing score was 70. My driver's license was issued on June 4, 2003, less than two weeks before my internship at the *Post* began. It would expire on February 3, 2011, the exact date of my thirtieth birthday. This Oregon license would be my only piece of government-issued identification for eight years. Meaning, I had eight years to "earn" being a "citizen."

When I look back now, I am stunned that not one person

during that entire period wondered if we were doing the right thing. There was a part of me that expected someone—maybe Rich, maybe Pat—to ask: "Are we breaking the law here?" Not once did someone say, "Wait, let's pause, let's think this through, this may get sticky." Not once.

When I arrived at the *Post* on June 2, 2004, for a full-time position, I knew I had to do everything I could to be "successful." In addition to the constant deadlines of newspaper reporting, there was a bigger personal deadline: February 3, 2011, the date my license would expire. It was a delicate dance: standing out in a highly competitive newsroom but not standing out so much as to draw attention and attract unwanted scrutiny. There was no room for error; I could not make any mistakes. There was also no room for enemies. I had to make friends and allies, but I had to make sure I didn't get too close to anyone or share more information than needed. I had to be careful.

I started freaking out about four months into the job, getting paranoid to the point of paralysis. It was one thing to risk being undocumented at the *San Francisco Chronicle*. It was a whole other thing to be undocumented at the *Washington Post*, hiding in plain sight in the nation's capital, where immigration was a constant topic of conversation. I was nervous, and it showed.

As the days and weeks passed, I walked around the newsroom like I had the word "ILLEGAL" tattooed on my forehead. It was getting harder and harder to focus on the work, and it became clear that I had to either leave the *Post* or find someone reliable who would keep my secret. As the years went by, as I kept on passing as an American, sharing my story was a compulsion, a way of relieving myself of the burden of the lies I had to tell so I could exist.

When I got back to my desk after lunch on October 27, 2004, I started looking at the website of the *Globe and Mail*, a newspaper in Canada. I had read that Canada had a friendlier immigration policy. Perhaps it was time to leave. After all, I can be a journalist anywhere in the world, I reassured myself. Maybe I was risking too much, as Lolo had warned. I couldn't just compartmentalize what I was feeling, as Rich had suggested two years before. Now was the time to tell somebody I could trust, in the same way I trusted Mrs. Denny, and Pat and Rich.

In my years of reporting, I'd developed a good sense of people, needing to size up potential sources quickly, whom to trust and whom to stay away from. Using the *Post*'s internal messaging system, I pinged Peter Perl.

I first met Peter when I was a summer intern. Every intern was randomly assigned a "professional partner"—a mentor— and he was mine. Peter started working at the *Post* in 1981, the year I was born.

Sitting on a bench across from the White House, I told Peter about everything. All of it. The license I wasn't supposed to get. The fake green card. The help I got from Pat, Rich, Mary, and Jim. I told Peter that years ago, after I found out I was here illegally, Lolo took me to the local Social Security Administration office to apply for a Social Security number, which I needed if I was to get any kind of job. To apply, we used a fake passport with my name on it that Lolo had bought. When the Social Security card arrived, it clearly stated: "Valid for work only with I.N.S. authorization." Lolo took me to a nearby Kinko's. He covered the "I.N.S. authorization" text with a sliver of white tape, and we made twenty or so photocopies of the doctored card. That photocopied, doctored card, I told Peter, is what I had submitted to the *Post*'s human resources department.

After my disclosure, I braced myself. I wasn't sure how Peter was going to react.

"I understand you a hundred times better now," Peter said. "This is now our shared problem."

Peter said that I had done the right thing by telling him, and that he didn't want to do anything about it just yet. I had just been hired, he said, and I needed to prove myself. When you've done enough, he went on, we'll tell the higher-ups.

A month later, I spent my first Thanksgiving in Washington with Peter and his family. To my surprise, the generosity of strangers that I'd been fortunate to find at Mountain View High School extended nearly three thousand miles to the Shapiro-Perl household in Silver Spring, Maryland.

14

CAMPAIGN 2008

"Young man," the sheriff said as he leaned against my rental car. "Did you know you were driving about thirty miles over the speed limit?" He took off his sunglasses. "License and registration, please."

It was March 2008. This was the first time I was pulled over by any kind of law enforcement. Usually, I was more than cautious, driving at or below the speed limit. But I was on deadline, working on a breaking news story on an election night, and I did not realize I was driving that fast. And of all the places to get caught, I was pulled over in Texas, an immigration battleground because it borders Mexico. I'd been driving for the past two weeks covering the historic primary race between Barack Obama and Hillary Clinton. As I slowly reached for my license, questions bounced around in my head. What if the sheriff finds out that I'm not supposed to have this license? What if he puts me through some test and I forget the address that's listed on the license? If he calls immigration on me, if I get arrested on the spot, do I get a phone call? What do I tell my editor at the newspaper, who is waiting on me to turn in an article, which is already late?

The sheriff's cell phone rang.

As he walked away from my car to answer the call, I felt something wet trickling down my pants.

I peed myself.

"I gotta head back to the station," the sheriff said. "I'm gonna let you go. Slow down, young man."

Slow down.

I had more than one deadline: the deadline for the news article I had to write and the deadline for the driver's license, which was set to expire.

There was no slowing down.

I froze as he drove away, and the stench of urine filled the car. Since procuring a license I wasn't supposed to have, driving had always been stressful. One way I dealt with the tension was by playing Stevie Wonder's "Don't You Worry 'Bout a Thing," which turned out to be the soundtrack of the two years I traveled the country covering the 2008 campaign. I was witnessing and covering American history, yet I felt like I had no right to be here.

Driving down Highway 175 that night in Texas, as Stevie was reminding me not to worry about a thing, I couldn't help but worry about everything.

Even when it seemed like everything was going well, really well, I worried about everything.

15

FACING MYSELF

My relationships with people were shaped by the secrets I kept and the lies I had to tell; I feared that the more I shared of myself, the more people I would drag into my mess.

The lies I told to get jobs were exacerbated by the lies I told friends and coworkers about who I was, where I came from, what I could not do, and why.

When my friend Angelica invited me to her wedding in Mexico City, I made up some lie about my grandmother being sick. For me, traveling outside of the country was out of the question. If I leave the U.S., there's no guarantee I would be allowed back.

I never displayed photos of family members at work or at home. You put photos up, people ask questions.

It was easier to say that I was alone, just as, years earlier, it was easier for me to represent myself at parent-teacher meetings.

For more than a decade, I carried the weight of trying to succeed in my profession—I need that byline, I need that story, I need to be seen—while wanting to be invisible so I didn't draw too much attention to myself.

Throughout 2010, I started reading stories about young undocumented Americans, many of them still in high school and college. Their rallying cry was: "We're undocumented, unafraid, and unapologetic." And using Facebook, Twitter, and YouTube, they were chronicling their own stories, daring politicians and the public alike to look away. I was particularly attracted to the story of a young undocumented immigrant from Ecuador named Maria Gabriela Pacheco, whom everyone called Gaby. She had been organizing for immigrant rights since she was in high school. Joined by three friends, Gaby walked from Miami, where she grew up, to Washington to drum up support for the DREAM Act. I followed Gaby's story on social media. I even stalked her on Facebook. There she was in the news, sharing her story publicly and trying to engage people like Joe Arpaio, the notorious sheriff who talked about and treated undocumented immigrants like cattle. How could she be so fearless? Why was I so scared?

For my life to go on, I had to get at the truth about where I came from. I realized that I could no longer live with my lies. Passing as a citizen was no longer enough. Before I could write any more stories, I had to investigate my life.

To free myself—in fact, to face myself—I had to write my story.

On June 22, 2011, the *New York Times Magazine* published "My Life as an Undocumented Immigrant." The essay's other headline: "OUTLAW."

A couple of days before my essay was scheduled to be published, I was at the *Times* building in Manhattan, going over the printed proofs of the essay, double-checking every fact, rereading every sentence. Since I've lied about so many facts about my life so I could pass as an American, the last thing I needed was any kind of correction. The essay had to be airtight.

My phone rang. It was one of the immigration lawyers who had been advising me. As a courtesy, I had sent a copy of the essay to the lawyers.

"Jose, are you going to print that you've done things that are 'unlawful'? In the *New York Times*?"

"Yes. It's in the essay."

"Jose, the moment you publish that, we cannot help you.

"Jose, are you there?"

She took a big breath.

Telling the truth—admitting that I had lied on government forms to get jobs—meant that now, trying to get citizenship legally would be nearly impossible.

I took a big breath.

"If I can't admit that, then why am I doing this?"

Publishing the essay, I realized, was breaking a cardinal rule in journalism: *write* the story, don't *be* the story. And, for more than a decade, I had already broken another cardinal rule of journalism—don't lie. For the record, I never lied in any of my stories. I never fabricated a single fact or contextual detail or made up a source. Still, I lied about who I am, specifically my legal status, a defining element of my life. To get jobs, I had lied to employers, from the *Chronicle* to the *HuffPost*, about my citizenship status. The essay was meant to right that wrong, to trace the origins of those lies, an attempt at getting at the "how" and "why." Why did I have to lie? How does someone become "illegal"?

Writing the essay was also journalism. Against the advice of lawyers—all of whom counseled me to not reveal this or that detail—I wrote it because I believed that its journalistic service to the public good was worth more than my personal need for legal protection. Yes, my life in this country was based on lies. Yes, I needed to pass as an American and as a U.S. citizen so I could work. But my journalism has always been grounded in truth since I covered that fire near the street I grew up on, and being a journalist is an identity I wear with deep pride.

16

PUBLIC PERSON, PRIVATE SELF

I've never considered myself an activist. In fact, I wasn't sure I knew the word's exact definition, so I looked it up. According to Merriam-Webster, "activist" is both a noun and an adjective. An "activist" is "a person who uses or supports strong actions (such as public protests) in support of or opposition to one side of a controversial issue." Whatever the definition, and leaving aside what I personally support or oppose, my essay about being undocumented was considered a form of activism by people from the political left and the right.

As immigration lawyers had warned me months before, revealing my undocumented status in such a highly visible way would render me unemployable. I had to worry about making money to support myself and my family, since Mama and my siblings in the Philippines depended on a monthly allowance that I'd been providing for years. My sister, Czarina, who was attending her last year of college, was especially worried. *"Kuya,"* she asked me on the phone, *"pwede pa rin ba akong makatapos ng kolehiyo?"* ("Older brother, can I still finish college?") Though I'd saved up some money that I could live on for a few months, it ran out sooner than I had planned for. By March 2012, nine months after my public disclosure, I had $250.84 left in my checking account and $66.74 in savings. If my friends had not lent me some money, I would not have made it. One of my best friends transferred money to my Bank of America account so I could make rent. It took a few more months to come up with a creative *and* legal solution. Forming my own organization would allow me to apply my skills to help rewrite the master narrative of immigration. And because I was no longer employable, being an undocumented entrepreneur would allow me to work within the confines of the law.

The moment my forty-three-hundred-word confessional was posted online, Define American was born. Cofounded with a close group of friends (Jake Brewer, one of the early innovators in online advocacy and organizing; Jehmu Greene, the former head of nonprofit groups Rock the Vote and Women's Media Center; and Alicia Menendez, a journalist and policy expert who knew more about the ins and outs of immigration than Jake, Jehmu, and I combined did), Define American is unlike anything else in the immigrant rights space. Our tactics, from the outset, have focused on neither policy nor politics. Taking a page from the playbook of the LGBTQ rights movement, we believe that you cannot change the politics of immigration until you change the culture in which immigrants are seen. Storytelling is central to our strategy: collecting stories of immigrants from all walks of life, creating original content (documentaries, databases, graphics, etc.), and leveraging stories we've collected and stories we've told to influence how news and entertainment media portray immigrants, both documented and undocumented. If you're a reporter looking for an undocumented mother who's taken sanctuary in a church, you can come to us. If you're a producer of a TV medical drama looking for stories of undocumented doctors to integrate in your show, you can contact us. Our #FactsMatter campaign combats every myth and answers every question you have about immigration. We have a #WordsMatter campaign that combats anti-immigrant speech and rhetoric that are rampant in all forms of media. Inspired by the Gay Straight Alliance movement that grew around the time I came out as gay in high school, we started a "chapters program" whose members consist of undocumented students and their U.S. citizen classmates. There are almost 60 chapters in college campuses in 26 states plus D.C.

Immediately after my essay was posted online and shared on social media, I became a public figure. After sharing my story, it was no longer mine—people dissected my story in whatever way they wanted. I was no longer just a person; I was now an "issue." I'm invited to appear on news shows and get recognized in public. I am targeted by people who want me to be detained and deported.

On any given day, people who've seen me on Fox News or read about me on conservative sites like Breitbart News, the *Daily Caller*, and Newsmax send private and public messages demanding my arrest and deportation. In the first days and weeks of the Trump presidency, tweets like "Christmas came early this year. It will be even earlier next year when @joseiswriting becomes Deportee #1" and "Hope your bags are packed @joseiswriting" started flooding my Twitter feed.

Once news reports began circulating that officers from Immigration and Customs Enforcement are targeting "high-profile illegal immigrants," a slew of messages landed on my feed, most from commenters who don't use their real names or real photos on their profiles. Usually, I ignore them. But this tweet from John Cardillo, host of a daily show, *America Talks Live*, on Newsmax, and whose account is verified by Twitter, was hard to ignore:

Hey @joseiswriting,

Tick tock

"ICE Detains Illegal Immigrant Activists."

Often, I ignore the tweets, Facebook messages, and emails. To deal with how personal people online can get, how cutting and revolting their language is, I've thought of myself as the subject of a news story. I try, as hard as I can, to look at the hateful words and the deplorable phrases with distance and detachment. They're not talking about me. They don't even know me. This "illegal alien" person they're describing with such vulgarity is someone else. It's not me.

And sometimes the people who follow me on Twitter and watch me on Fox News are not at all who I think they are, in the same way that I'm not who they think I am.

"Is it you? Are you the 'illegal' guy on Fox?" said the tall, middle-aged white man in khakis and a striped white shirt and oversize black coat. He and I were standing in the Delta Air Lines terminal at Tampa International Airport, waiting to board a flight to LaGuardia Airport. It was February 2015. I had just given a speech at the Black, Brown & College Bound Summit for African American and Latino students at a hotel in downtown Tampa. I was headed to New York City for meetings.

Sometimes, because of TV appearances, I get recognized in public, mostly at airports and Starbucks. It's been about

70–30: Most people are supportive, and many of them "come out" to me as undocumented. Some get a little aggressive, asking why I have still not gotten deported. More often than not, I engage in conversations. But I was too tired to engage that afternoon in Tampa. Instead of answering, I half nodded, then walked away, lugging my carry-on bag.

I've spent more time in airports and planes than in whatever apartment I was living at. I changed apartments four times in the past seven years (New York City; Washington, D.C.; San Francisco; Los Angeles), as I traveled to countless cities and towns in forty-eight states, doing more than a thousand events: speaking at panels, giving speeches, visiting schools, meeting with all kinds of people from all backgrounds. I fly so much, especially on Delta Air Lines and American Airlines, that I often get upgraded to first class, as I was that afternoon.

A few seconds after I boarded the plane, as I was stowing my luggage, the white man in the oversize black coat grabbed my left shoulder as he walked by. "I didn't know illegals fly first class," he said.

I sat down. I wasn't sure if anyone else heard him, but the woman clutching her iPad across the aisle must have seen my face. I was upset. I'd been used to all the words, but that was the first time I had been touched, and I didn't know how to react. I felt violated. I was mad. I put on my headset and tried to get lost in my thoughts with Ella Fitzgerald and Joni Mitchell. That didn't work. A few minutes later, after the flight had taken off, I stood up and headed to the bathroom, even though I did not need to go to the bathroom. I wanted to see where he was sitting, which was near the middle of the plane, in a middle seat between two women. He didn't see me looking at him. At least I don't think he did.

What was his story? Why did he think it was okay to grab me like that? Did it make him feel good? Feel better, stronger? Superior? What was going through his mind when he decided that his hand should land on my shoulder? What else did he want to say? What else did he want to do?

And what should I do?

I bought Wi-Fi access and got on my personal Facebook page, which only my friends and relatives can see. I summarized what happened and ended the post with: "This is gonna be an awkward flight."

"Awkward for whom?" wrote my friend Tricia. "You're the one flying in style while he gets coach. As it should be."

I wish I could listen to my friend Glenn, who wrote: "You upset him, just by being yourself and doing the right thing. You win! Don't give him one more thought or one more second of your time."

This wasn't about winning or losing, and I couldn't stop thinking about him in that middle seat. I'm a big guy and his shoulders were bigger than mine. Not fun for the middle seat.

Todd chimed in: "Ask the flight attendant to send back some champagne to him and watch his head explode."

Should I tell the flight attendant?

I didn't know what to do until I read what Graciela wrote: "So you're in First Class and he's not? Sounds perfect."

After reading that comment, after I realized the irony of the situation—"the illegal riding first class"—I decided to talk to the guy.

Once we landed at LaGuardia International Airport, I grabbed my bags and waited for him to get out of the plane. He was surprised to see me waiting outside the terminal.

"I'm Jose," I said.

"Eric." I asked if it was Eric with a "c" or Eric with a "k," and it was the former. He wouldn't give me his last name.

I told him that I got upgraded to first class because I travel so much. The upgrade, I said, was free.

"Must be nice," Eric said.

"Yes, it is," I said, feeling upset at myself for wanting to explain myself. I don't owe this guy an explanation. Why am I talking to him?

"Look, I didn't mean to seem like a jerk. I've seen you on TV. Bragging."

"Bragging about what?"

"Being illegal."

I told Eric that it wasn't something I brag about. It's not something I'm proud of. It's something I want to fix, and that there's no way to fix it.

"You want to get legal?"

"Of course. Why would I want to be like this?"

"Oh."

He lives in New Jersey, right outside of Trenton. He said he was forty-eight, and he had just gotten laid off from his job at an insurance company, where he had worked for almost a decade. He's divorced with two kids, both teenagers. After about fifteen minutes of conversation, as we made our way into the baggage claim area, he felt the need to point out that he voted for Obama twice. I told him Obama had deported more immigrants than any other modern president, a fact that seemed to surprise him.

"Politics," he said, shrugging.

I gave him my business card and wrote DefineAmerican .com/facts on the back of it. That site, I told him, has all the facts he would ever need to know about immigration. I wanted to ask him if he knew where his ancestors came from, if he knew what papers they had when they moved to America. But I didn't. I told him I needed to go, and we parted ways. I've yet to hear from him on email.

Because I am public about my undocumented status, there are people who decide to appoint themselves as immigration officials, questioning why I'm here.

In May 2018, I was invited to speak at a conference about stress in kids. The gathering took place at MIT, and I'd never been surrounded by so many pediatricians, researchers, and scientists, all grappling with how to study and combat what everybody was calling "toxic stress." I participated in a panel. About a hundred people were in the room. Some people had either seen me on TV or heard my story. Some people had not. After my brief talk, a middle-aged woman sitting in the middle of the room raised her hand. She looked like she was South Asian.

"I find your comments very offensive, because we are immigrants, we came legally to this country, we followed all the rules," she said, looking me straight in the eye.

I could feel the room's temperature heighten.

The woman continued.

"You should not group together legal and illegal immigrants because we followed every rule that the U.S. told us to follow. We didn't break any laws and we entered this country legally."

A young woman was seated directly in front of the older South Asian woman. She looked increasingly uncomfortable, eventually appearing to melt into her seat. I thought I heard some people gasp. Others looked at me in horror.

The older woman went on, her voice rising.

"You've broken the laws of this country! Don't bind legal with illegal. We are different. We are not you."

At that point, I jumped in. Don't lose your cool, I started telling myself. Don't yell. Don't get mad. Don't lose your cool.

"I hear this a lot, and it's really important that we address it. Out of thirty-four people in my Filipino American family, I'm the only one who's undocumented. So, you cannot separate the 'legal' from the 'illegal,'" I said. "And, by the way, I am here illegally, but as a human being, I cannot be illegal because that doesn't exist. People cannot be illegal."

She cut me off.

"You had a chance to become legal because of amnesty."

"Which was in 1986," I interjected. "I came here in 1993."

One of the organizers intervened and said the conversation was off topic. I wanted to keep going. I wanted to show everyone in the room that when it comes to immigration, the ignorance and indifference are everywhere, across political parties. They were right here at MIT.

After the panel, the attendees started spilling out of the room. I looked for the woman and found her. She wouldn't give me her name. She said she emigrated from India and that she became a U.S. citizen because of her husband. She also told me that she was an immigration lawyer. I was floored. If an immigration lawyer was foggy on the history of America's immigration policies, then who could be expected to keep it straight? She was condemning me for not following a process that didn't exist, which I will explain more later. Breathe, I told myself. Breathe in. Breathe out. Find compassion for this woman.

She told me that she thought the resources that were going

to "illegals" should be going to blacks. "They're Americans," she said. "You're not."

I gave her my business card and walked away, feeling tired of carrying the burden of having to explain myself every day.

17

MY GOVERNMENT, MYSELF

I am not hiding from my government. My government is hiding from me.

At least that's how it's felt in the past seven years since my essay was published, living a public life as undocumented. The only way I've been able to survive the discomfort and distress of the past seven years is by doing what Mrs. Dewar at Mountain View High School said I was good at: asking questions.

"Are you planning on deporting me?" I asked the immigration officer on the phone.

It was May 2012. I prepared myself for the worst after publicly declaring my undocumented status: possible arrest and detention, at any time of any day. The only thing I didn't prepare for was silence. Especially from the government. Particularly the folks from Immigration and Customs Enforcement (ICE), which had removed nearly four hundred thousand individuals from the country in fiscal year 2011, which ended September 30, 2011—exactly one hundred days after I outed myself in the *New York Times*. In 2010, nearly 393,000 immigrants were deported. A year before that, almost 390,000 people. John Morton, who led ICE, touted the 2011 deportation numbers, calling them the result of "smart and effective immigration enforcement" that depended on "setting clear priorities for removal and executing on those priorities."

"I haven't heard from you," I said to the officer as I introduced myself. I told her I was done hiding. I confessed how anxious I was that I'd heard nothing from ICE, nothing from the Department of Homeland Security, nothing from the Department of Justice.

The officer, who was working at the ICE branch in New York City, where I was living at the time, was confused. She said she knew who I was.

"Why are you calling us?" she said.

"Because I want to know what you want to do with me."

"What are you doing?"

"What are *you* doing?"

The agent placed me on hold.

A few days after the new year in 2013, I heard from the government—but not from anyone in Immigration and Customs Enforcement. The call was from the office of Senator Patrick Leahy of Vermont. His office asked me to testify as part of the latest push to pass immigration reform. President Obama was in office, and it was a priority for him to pass a set of laws to regulate immigration into the U.S. President Obama couldn't have won the White House without the Latino vote in 2008 and 2012, but he did not tackle the issue of immigration in his first year in office, when Democrats controlled both the House and the Senate. Since I couldn't wrangle any answers from the immigration officer on the phone, I wanted to take my questions directly to congressional members. After all, two of the country's most anti-immigrant senators, Jeff Sessions and Ted Cruz, sat on the judiciary committee, which is in charge of laws regulating immigration, among many other things. Janet Napolitano, who headed the Department of Homeland Security, was also asked to testify. To my mind, nothing says *I am done hiding from my government* more than appearing before Congress. I wanted to make it a family affair, given how special it is to testify in front of Congress.

I don't recall ever being as nervous as I was on the day of the hearing. Writing the testimony, which couldn't be longer than five minutes, was daunting enough. I felt prepared to answer whatever questions they lobbed at me. The source of anxiety came from the terror of losing my composure and breaking down. In front of congressional members. In front of my family. In front of other undocumented immigrants, who started piling into the hearing room.

"I come to you as one of our country's eleven million undocumented immigrants, many of us Americans at heart, but without the right papers to show for it," I began.

Lola sat behind me. I was sure I could hear her heart beating. I was so overwhelmed by the row of photographers, I didn't dare look at them.

"Too often, we're treated as abstractions, faceless and nameless, subjects of debate rather than individuals with families, hopes, fears, and dreams," I went on, continuing to tell my story. The lies I had to tell so I could pass as an American. The sacrifices of my family: Lolo, Lola, and Mama, especially Mama. The generosity of Pat, Rich, and Jim, underscoring the all-too-forgotten reality that "there are countless other Jim Strands, Pat Hylands, and Rich Fischers of all backgrounds who stand alongside their undocumented neighbors," who don't need "pieces of paper—a passport or a green card—to treat us as human beings." I wasn't the only one who was done hiding. They were done hiding, too.

As I headed for the last few sentences of my prepared remarks, I grabbed my copy of President Kennedy's *A Nation of Immigrants.* The book's foreword was written by Ted Kennedy, his younger brother who fought for the passage of the 1965 Immigration and Nationality Act and, in turn, fought for immigration reform arguably harder than anyone else in the Senate. My family got here because of the 1965 law. I had hidden from Kennedy, too. While I was a reporter for the *Washington Post*, I interviewed him in Albuquerque in February 2008, a few days after he endorsed Obama for president. I wanted to tell him I was undocumented. I wanted to ask him for help. But I chickened out. I was not chickening out today.

I went off script.

"Before I take your questions here, I have a few of my own: What do you want to do with me?

"For all the undocumented immigrants who are actually sitting at this hearing, for all the people watching online, and for the eleven million of us: What do you want to do with us?

"And to me, the most important question, as a student of American history, is this: How do you define 'American'?"

As I ended my remarks, the only senator to ask a question was Sessions.

"Mr. Vargas, would you agree fundamentally that a great nation should have an immigration policy and then create a legal system that carries that policy out and then enforces that policy?"

"Yes, sir."

That was it. Faced with a real person, "a criminal alien," in his words, the kind whom he regularly describes as if he's talking about fungus in his toenail, that was his only question. Ted Cruz, a senator from Texas who also wanted strict immigration laws, wasn't even around that day; I don't think he heard the testimony. The silence from the other Republican senators who oppose any sort of "immigration reform," any real solution, reminded me of the silence from the immigration officer I had called just a few months before.

I would find out that even though I publicly declared my undocumented status—on the phone, on TV shows, in front of Congress—I still did not exist in the eyes of ICE. Like most undocumented immigrants, I'd never been arrested. I'd been so careful not to get arrested. And that meant I'd never been in contact with ICE.

After all the years of lying, after all the years of trying to pass as an American, after all the anxiety, the uncertainty, the confusion, the only response I could get from the United States government, courtesy of the ICE agent who put me hold, was: "No comment."

How do you build a life with "no comment"?

I waved my hands in front of ICE. I testified in front of Congress. I tried to get answers. But nothing. I live in fear of what can happen, knowing that I can get detained and deported at any time.

18

NATIONAL SECURITY THREAT

In the summer of 2014, Cristina Jiménez of United We Dream, a national youth-led immigrant rights organization, sent me a text message, asking if Define American would be interested in joining a delegation traveling to McAllen, Texas, in the Rio Grande Valley.

The goal of the trip, Cristina said, was to organize a vigil welcoming arriving Central American refugees, most of whom were children fleeing for their lives. Many traveled alone, a journey of hundreds of miles by trains, buses, and on foot just to get across the Rio Grande.

Whether you call them migrants, immigrants, or refugees, their journeys included an arduous trek through blistering desert terrain. Often, they lacked food, water, and shelter. Many arrived dehydrated and hungry. Some required medical attention. Once they crossed the Rio Grande, they didn't try to hide from Border Patrol agents. They walked up to the officers and gave themselves up.

I wasn't sure if I should fly to Texas. I was not a refugee. I wondered if my showing up there would take attention away from their plight. But the more I read about what was happening in McAllen, the more I wanted to go. My plan was to fly in, participate in the vigil, help a friend of mine film the vigil, and fly out. I'd never been to southern Texas. My only experience of being close to the border was in Southern California, where some of my relatives live. The Texas border was a whole other experience, a militarized area swarming with Border Patrol agents, Department of Public Safety officers, and immigration officials. Along the three-mile drive from the McAllen Miller International Airport, where I was picked up, to my hotel, I counted seven Border Patrol cars, just driving around. Nearby, a Department of Public Safety helicopter hovered. At the Starbucks not too far from the hotel, many of the customers were uniformed agents and officers on their breaks.

When my friend Mony, an immigration lawyer who used to work in the area, saw on my Facebook page that I was in McAllen, she texted me: "I am so glad you are visiting the kids near the border. But how will you get through the checkpoint on your way back?" A curious question, I thought, and one I dismissed. I've visited the border before, in California. What checkpoint? What was she talking about?

Soon, I realized that flying out of McAllen won't be nearly as easy as flying into McAllen. There are checkpoints everywhere, including the airport. When I told Cristina about the situation, her eyes widened. "Oh my God, Jose! I forgot you don't have DACA!" DACA is short for Deferred Action for Childhood Arrivals, an immigration policy that allows immigrants who were brought to the U.S. illegally as children to apply for temporary status. Unlike the DREAM Act, DACA does not lead to a path to citizenship, but it does authorize people to legally work. When DACA was introduced in 2012, I was about four months too old to qualify for it.

At the Texas border, "border security" is an inescapable daily reality, a reminder of where you cannot go, what your limitations are. "Border security" means running random checkpoints anywhere within one hundred miles of the U.S.-Mexico border, a Constitution-free zone in which agents can stop your car, inspect your belongings, and ask for your papers, regardless of your immigration status. (The Fourth Amendment does not allow for citizens to be subjected to random search and seizures, but in the interest of "national security," the Fourth Amendment does not apply within a hundred miles of the border.) For residents of the Rio Grande Valley who are undocumented, or who are U.S. citizens but live with parents or siblings who are undocumented, "border security" means knowing you can't drive for more than half an hour south, no more than an hour and a half east, and no more than two hours north.

Soon, Cristina was strategizing on how I could leave McAllen quietly and discreetly. She'd invited me thinking I had DACA, and she kept apologizing for not remembering that I didn't have it. "We need to get you out," she texted. "We can drive you to SA." San Antonio. Someone suggested hiding me in the trunk so I could get through the checkpoint.

The moment that suggestion was made—hide? in the trunk?—I knew in my heart that I had to stay. I decided to continue what I've been doing since I stopped hiding who I am. I wrote an essay that was published on the website *Politico* the following day:

"I write this from the city of McAllen. . . . In the last 24 hours I realize that, for an undocumented immigrant like me, getting out of a border town in Texas—by plane or by land—won't be easy. It might, in fact, be impossible."

The headline: "Trapped on the Border."

Some people thought the whole thing was a stunt, but it was an accident. I didn't know I was going to be cornered there. I had to call Lola and assure her everything would be fine. I drafted an email to my loved ones and explained what was happening and what could happen. After consulting with immigration lawyers, we decided that I would leave McAllen in the same way I arrived: by plane. A wealthy friend offered to get me a private plane, which I thought was a joke until he assured me it wasn't. I declined the offer and said I wanted to fly out how I flew in.

I flew into McAllen from the John F. Kennedy International Airport in New York City, where I used my Philippine passport—the only piece of acceptable identification I had at the time—to get through security. Like all the other airports across the country that I had flown into and out of, there was no Border Patrol agent checking papers of domestic travelers at JFK. The McAllen airport was different. At the McAllen airport, a Border Patrol agent would stand next to the TSA agent checking everyone's papers. So, as I waited in line, I inserted my Philippine passport inside my pocketbook copy of the Declaration of Independence and U.S. Constitution, as if that act provided some sort of protection. My heart pounded in my chest as I approached the agents, as my mind cataloged every possible outcome.

A TSA agent checked my passport and compared it to my plane ticket. Then a Border Patrol agent took my passport from the TSA agent and flipped it open.

"Do you have your visa?" the agent asked.

"No, there's no visa," I replied matter-of-factly, as if I

was writing a news article and answering the question for someone else.

The moment he asked, "Are you here illegally?" I reminded myself that it was me he was talking to.

Without any hesitation, I answered with a clipped "Yes."

Then, in a clear voice drenched in defiance, I added: "I am."

19

DETAINED

Of all the ways I imagined the inevitable, I never envisioned sitting on the cold cement floor of a jail cell in south Texas surrounded by children.

The cell, as I remember it, was no bigger than twenty feet by thirty feet. All around me were about twenty-five boys, as young as five years old, the oldest no more than twelve. The air reeked of body odor. A boy across the room from me was crying inconsolably, his head buried on his chest. I tried to make eye contact to no avail. Most of the boys wore dazed expressions. It was clear they had no idea where they were or why they were there.

The only source of wonder came from Mylar blankets, the flimsy metallic sheets that were supposed to keep us warm, the same blankets that were first used in outer space, which must be as desolate as this cell. By the look of it, the boys had never seen these blankets before and didn't know what to do with them. Three boys played with a blanket like it was a toy, crunching it up into a ball, passing it back and forth.

A window faced a central area where a dozen or so patrol agents were stationed, but there was no view of the outside world. All I could do was stare at the boys' shoes. My shoes were shiny and brand-new, theirs dirty, muddy, and worn down. The only thing our shoes had in common was that none of them had laces.

"Jose Antonio Vargas," said an agent as he walked in.

Startled, I sprung up, unsure why my name was being called.

"I don't need you. Not yet," the agent said. "But we're gonna move you."

Before he could hear me ask why, the agent shut the door as another detainee, a young woman with a wide-eyed baby on her hip, walked by, unaccompanied.

The moment the agent said my name, one of the boys playing with a blanket started speaking to me. I had no idea what he was saying. The one word I could make out was *"miedo."* Something about *"miedo."*

If I spoke Spanish, I could have told the boys not to be scared.

If I spoke Spanish, I could have told the boys about Ellis Island. About how the very first person in line on the opening day of America's first immigration station—an unaccompanied minor named Annie Moore who traveled on a steamship from Ireland—was someone just like them. Except she was white, before she knew she was white.

If I spoke Spanish, I could have told the boys that none of this was their fault. I could have made sure they understood—even if most Americans do not—that people like us come to America because America was in our countries.

I could have explained, in the clearest way I could, the connection between the actions of the United States of America and the reactions in their countries of birth. How the largest groups of people who migrate to the U.S.A.—voluntarily, forcibly, unknowingly, like them—do so because of the relationship between the U.S. and other countries. A trade agreement, like the North American Free Trade Agreement, hurt the Mexican economy, especially local farmers and small business owners. People lost jobs, leading parents to cross the U.S. border so they could feed their kids. For decades, the U.S. government interfered with and influenced the governments of El Salvador, Guatemala, and Honduras in ways that created instability and sowed violence. All the while, U.S. companies exported products to those countries to grow their businesses, and they were so successful that young boys inside the cell were wearing dirty, muddy, worn-out Reeboks and Nikes. Reeboks and Nikes could come to Honduras, but young Hondurans wearing Reeboks and Nikes were not welcome to the U.S.

I don't understand Spanish. The only Spanish thing about me is my name. Aside from asking *"Dondé esta la biblioteca?"* ("Where is the library?"), one of a few phrases I know is *"No hablo español."* ("I don't speak Spanish.") I told the boy: *"No hablo español."* Quickly, I added, *"Soy filipino."* I am Filipino: a declaration that seemed to cause more confusion to the young boy holding the crunched-up blanket. I'm not sure he heard me when I said, almost in a whisper, like a prayer, *"Pepeton ang pangalan ko."* My name is Pepeton.

It's my nickname, combining the nicknames of Jose (Pepe) and Antonio (Ton). But it's more than a sobriquet, more than a term of endearment. It's the name of my past: what Mama and everyone in the Philippines who knows me calls me. It's the name I don't tell people about, certainly not after I found out I was in America without proper documents. It's the name I've avoided so I could construct a different kind of identity, not the "illegal immigrant" you see and hear about in the news, but a successful journalist who breaks news and writes about the news. It's the name I've escaped from so I could escape whatever and whoever I needed to escape: my past and Mama, the U.S. government, myself. But there was no place to hide now, nothing to run away from, no role to play.

All I could see as I stared at the boys was young Pepeton staring me back.

20

ALONE

The agents inside the sixty-eight-thousand-square-foot McAllen Border Patrol Station on West Military Highway did not know what to do with me.

They kept moving me from one cell to another. An agent took me out of the cell with the boys and put me in a much smaller one by myself. Then back again with the boys, then back again to the cell by myself. I realized that I was separated from the other men, who were locked up in different cells. I walked past one cell that had only grown women—pregnant women, women cradling babies, women talking to one another.

Two hours passed before an agent opened the door and peeked his head in. "Are you famous or something?" He closed the door and seconds later opened it again. He held up his phone and showed me an article on CNN. "Dude, you're all over the news."

After I was handcuffed at the airport, I'd been driven alone in a white van. The ride to the station took less than fifteen minutes, if that. Upon my arrival, two agents took everything I had: my phone, my wallet, my backpack, my luggage. I was asked to take off my leather belt and the laces in my shoes. When I asked why, one of the agents said, "We don't want you hurting yourself."

I wanted to laugh out loud after the agent said that. I've always used laughter to conceal the pain; here, to distance and detach myself from the absurdity of this whole ordeal. Is this really about who has the right papers and what the laws are? Or is this about someone to control? Is this really about who is a citizen or not? Are we talking about the same citizenship that many Americans callously take for granted? Are these agents so blithely unaware that they and their government have hurt me more than I could ever hurt myself?

But I say nothing.

There was no bathroom in the cell. You had to call an agent to use one. Incredibly, I did not use the bathroom in the hours I was locked up. I managed to hold it in. I should have used the bathroom as an excuse to check out the rest of the station. That was what a curious and enterprising reporter would have done. But for the first time, I wasn't a reporter, which was the only thing I knew how to be, so long as I was reporting on other people and what was happening to them.

The quietness is forbidding, all alone in that cell. Nothing but you and your thoughts, which become somewhat tangible, bouncing around the white walls and the cold floors before building into some emotional squall. There was no place to run. No role to play. Though I was fully clothed, I'd never felt more naked in my whole life.

There was nowhere to run away from and no need to hurry. My life of deadlines came to a halt, the facts clearly in front of me. The father I never had, or who left me, the mother I left, or who left me. The country I left, which was my home, which I don't know much about, and the country I am in, which is my home, except it isn't. It's dangerous out there, and home should be the place where we feel safe and at peace.

Home is not something I should have to earn.

Humanity is not some box I should have to check.

I've never been in a long-term relationship. Never had a boyfriend. Never allowed anyone to get close. But it occurred to me that I'd been in an intimate, long-term relationship all along. I was in a toxic, abusive, codependent relationship with America, and there was no getting out.

The very reason that I'm locked up in this cell is because of who I am and who I've become. Who am I without

America? What would I be without America?

Sitting alone in that cell, I concluded that none of this was an accident. None of it. Politicians and the news media that cover them like to say that we have a "broken immigration system." Inside that cell I came to the conclusion that we do not have a broken immigration system. We don't. What we're doing—waving a "KEEP OUT!" flag at the Mexican border while holding up a HELP WANTED sign a hundred yards in—is deliberate. Spending billions building fences and walls, locking people up like livestock, deporting people to keep the people we don't want out, tearing families apart, breaking spirits—all of that serves a purpose. People are forced to lie, people spend years if not decades passing in some purgatory. And step by step, this immigration system is set up to do exactly what it does.

Dear America, is this what you really want? Do you even know what is happening in your name?

I don't know what else you want from us.

I don't know what else you need us to do.

21

INTERVIEW

"So, when did you arrive in the United States?"

After the sixth hour, I was taken out of the cell and escorted inside an office, where an agent asked me questions while he filled out a form. His name was Mario, and he was clean-shaven and looked like he had only been in this job for the past few months. He was of Mexican descent, like all the other agents in the station.

"August 3, 1993."

"Did you cross the border?"

"No. My border was the Pacific Ocean."

"Huh?"

"I'm from the Philippines."

He laughed. "Hey, I know someone from the Philippines. You guys have Mexican names." As he started talking about "Pac Man"—as in Manny Pacquiao, the famous Filipino boxer—I saw him place an accent on the "é" in "José." I stopped him and said that Filipinos, for reasons I don't fully understand, don't put accents on our Spanish names. "I guess it's our way of rebelling against Spanish colonialism. Or something like that." I might not be able to control what was happening, but I was going to control the punctuation of my name. It was a defense mechanism, also a way of distracting myself from the fact that I was losing control. As a journalist, usually I ask questions. I don't answer them.

Later, I would find out why my name doesn't carry an accent mark. After the Americans forced the Spanish out of the Philippines, American typewriters couldn't type accented vowels. My name is Jose because of Spanish colonialism. But Jose isn't José because of American imperialism. Even my name isn't really mine.

He broke the silence and asked: "Who did you come with? Your mom?"

"No. My mom put me on a plane."

"By yourself?"

"No. I was with this guy who my mom told me was an uncle."

"So, you came with your uncle."

"Actually, I found out later on that he wasn't my uncle. He was a stranger that my grandfather—my mama's dad—paid to get me here. My mother sent me to live with her parents—"

He cut me off. "You came with a coyote," he said. "A lot of the kids here had coyotes."

I nodded.

More silence.

Again, he broke it and asked: "What do you do?"

"I'm a journalist."

"Yeah. I know. I looked you up," he said. "Why journalist?"

"I don't know." By this point, I was annoyed and confused. He already knew I was a journalist, yet he asked the question just to stall the conversation, like he needed to buy some time. He kept looking at the window waiting for someone important to show up.

"You always wanted to be a journalist?"

"No. I wanted to make films." If he had looked even remotely interested, I would have said that I wanted to make films because it was a way of showing the world what you see. Films are a way of seeing beyond yourself, into other people and other places. Films are possibilities, both real and imagined.

Instead, I continued: "When I found out I was undocumented, that I didn't have the right kind of papers to be here, I wanted my name to be in the newspaper." If he really wanted to know, I would have said that having my name in the newspaper—"by Jose Antonio Vargas"—was the only way I could think of existing and contributing something concrete in the process. That was my article. I reported it. I wrote it. It's real. I'm real.

This time I broke the silence. "Why did you become a Border Patrol agent?"

"The benefits are solid, man."

Seconds later, another guard came into the room, the same guard who took my shoelaces and asked if I was famous. All afternoon, the guards I'd encountered had given me knowing looks, like I was a lab experiment they had figured out. If they had, they didn't tell me. Who was I? Who had I become? Where was I going? What they did say was that within an hour or so, I would be released, but they were trying to figure out how. I kept asking why I was being released. They wouldn't say. "There are a lot of reporters out there," the other guard said. "They're waiting for you." I asked if either of them spoke Spanish. They both did.

"What's *'miedo'*?"

"Fear," one of the agents said. "It means fear."

22

CYCLE OF LOSS

Sitting on the floor, staring at the boys in the cell, I kept thinking of their parents, the fear they must have felt knowing that they needed to do what they needed to do. I also kept thinking of my mother, wondering as I had so many times over all these years what she told herself as she said goodbye to me at that airport twenty-five years ago.

Mama and I rarely talked about what happened at the airport. Sometimes I would ask about a fact here or there. What was I wearing? What was she wearing? What were her last words to me? But we never talked about how we felt, what we lost, what it means. That's the truth, as hard as it may seem to believe. Maybe it's because it's too hard for me to ask and too painful for her to remember. Maybe it's because we both know it wouldn't change anything. Maybe it's because the truth is too heavy to carry around.

The truth is, I'm not the only one who lost a mother. Mama lost a mother, too. Lola, my mother's mother, left the Philippines and moved to America in 1984, three years after I was born. Lola had seen her only daughter, my mama, no more than six times in thirty-four years, quick visits of two to three weeks every few years. Mama is waiting in line to legally come to America. As the decades have passed, their relationship, like my relationship with Mama, is mostly measured by the American products that we ship over to the Philippines and the U.S. dollars that we provide that Mama can't live without. We think we can bury what we've lost under all the things we can buy. When the truth is, the loss that my mother can't express to her mother is what I struggle to express to her now. Lola and I have reconnected; my coming out as undocumented brought us closer together. I wish Lolo was still around. He died in 2007, and I was grateful that I had the opportunity to apologize to him for not understanding why he did what he did. I may not have understood his plans, but the truth is, his intention of giving me a better life was pure.

And the truth is, if Mama had known then what she knows

now—that calling her on the phone is difficult, because I can't really pretend that I know the voice on the other end of the line—that seeing her on Skype or FaceTime feels like some sort of twisted joke—that the technology that easily connects us makes the borders that divide us even more visible—I'm not sure if she would have said goodbye at the airport. On one of our rare phone calls she said, "I look at you, now, the person you've become, and how can I have any regrets?" I'm sure she meant it as a statement, but it sounded like a question.

The truth is, there's a part of me, I'm uncertain how much, who is still in that airplane, wondering why Mama put me there.

Mama will turn sixty-one this year. At thirty-seven, I am a year older than she was when she dropped me off at the airport on that hurried morning. I told her that since that morning, I've always been hurried, that working on this book is the first time I've ever allowed myself the space and time to feel, and that I'd been feeling lost and alone. When she asked me where I was, I said I was staying at a hotel. I told her I had no home at the moment: no physical space of my own, no permanent address.

"Maybe," Mama said, her voice growing fainter for a moment, "maybe it's time to come home."

23

LEAVING / STAYING

A few days before the inauguration of President Donald Trump, the building manager in the apartment complex I was living in—a nice guy named Mel, who cheered me on whenever he saw me on MSNBC, Fox News, or CNN—told me that if immigration agents showed up, he wasn't sure the building could hide me. He felt ashamed to say it, but tension had been building since the election. In a text message, Mel wrote: "It may be safer for you to move out." A lawyer friend of mine—I've collected a handful of lawyer friends since disclosing my status as an undocumented immigrant in 2011—suggested I prepare for the worst-case scenario: not only getting detained, but also getting deported. Having a permanent address means the government knows where to find me. When I relayed that my building manager had asked that I consider moving out for my own safety, another lawyer friend replied, "Well, the man has a point. It's not a good idea for you to have a permanent address."

All around me, everyone issued warnings and raised red flags, especially after Trump signed executive orders on immigration, further confusing an already chaotic enforcement system and declaring every "illegal" a priority for deportation.

One lawyer friend warned me against flying around the country, especially in the South and the Midwest. Another lawyer friend insisted that I stop flying even within California, since news was spreading that immigration agents were checking the immigration status of domestic passengers. "Can you just stay put in one place," a lawyer friend asked, "and not fly around the country?"

Another friend suggested, "What if you flew to Canada?"

I entertained the idea for about two weeks.

Three days after my birthday, on the morning of Monday, February 6, 2017, an email landed in my inbox. In all caps, its subject line read: "LEADER NANCY PELOSI INVITATION—JOINT SESSION OF CONGRESS."

Dear Jose,

Good morning! Leader Nancy Pelosi invites you to be her guest at the Joint Session of Congress by the President on Tuesday, February 28th, 2017 at the United States Capitol.

Pelosi's formal invitation put my predicament in sharp focus.

I came to the realization that I refuse to let a presidency scare me from my own country. I refuse to live a life of fear defined by a government that doesn't even know why it fears what it fears. Because I am not a citizen by law or by birth, I've had to create and hold on to a different kind of citizenship. I call it citizenship of participation. Citizenship is showing up. Citizenship is using your voice while making sure you hear other people around you. Citizenship is how you live your life.

I accepted the invitation, which meant going back to the Capitol, where I had not been since I testified in 2013. Once a year, the President of the United States of America drives up to the Capitol and delivers a speech to Congress. This speech was the first time President Trump addressed Congress—the same Trump who won the White House by depicting undocumented immigrants like me as a burden to society, dangerous and expendable. My attendance was my own way of exhibiting my citizenship. Even though it wasn't safe—I could get arrested just by entering the Capitol—it was the right thing for me to do. I wrote an essay for the *Washington Post*, which was published a few minutes after I entered the Capitol and sat down in the gallery of the House's hallowed chamber to watch Trump speak.

I explained why I showed up:

I decided to show up tonight because that's what immigrants, undocumented and documented, do: We show up. Despite the obvious risks and palpable fear, we show up to work, to school, to church, to our communities, in big cities and rural towns. We show up and we participate. This joint session of Congress is a quintessential American moment at a critical juncture in our history. I am honored to attend and remind our elected leaders and everyone watching that immigration, at its core, is about families and love—the sacrifices of our families, and the love that we feel for a country we consider our home although it labels us "aliens." We show up even though we're unwanted, even when most Americans don't understand . . . why we come here in the first place. . . . We show up even though many Americans, especially white Americans with

**their own immigrant backgrounds, can't seem
to see the common threads between why we
show up and why they showed up, at a time
when showing up did not require visas and the
Border Patrol didn't exist yet.**

After attending the joint session—and after many
conversations with lawyer friends—I moved out of my
apartment in Los Angeles. I put almost everything I own
in storage and started giving away furniture to relatives
and friends. For the first time since leaving Lolo and Lola's
house after my high school graduation, I don't have my own
apartment. I don't have a permanent address. I'm staying at
hotels, Airbnbs, and in spare bedrooms of close friends.

I've decided to keep my travel schedule as is, fully aware
of the possible consequences. I don't know if I'll be detained
again. I don't know when or if I will get deported. What I am
sure of, however, is that America is where I became whoever
I am, where I was welcomed by Americans who didn't need
pieces of paper or laws to treat me like I am a human being.
I may be undocumented, but I am a citizen of this country.

I am home.

ACKNOWLEDGMENTS

To me, books are miraculous, and the people who work in books—who bring life to book publishing—are miraculous people. Profound thanks to the awesome team at HarperCollins Children's Books: Mitchell Thorpe, Vaishali Nayak, Kimberly Stella, Vanessa Nuttry, Catherine San Juan, Erin Fitzsimmons, Jessica Berg, and Gwen Morton. Special shout-out to Alyssa Miele, who made sure I made every deadline, and Alexandra Cooper, whose idea it was in the first place to adapt my book into a children's book. I owe a great deal of gratitude to Jay Mandel and Jennifer Rudolph Walsh, my agents at WME.

I am a product of three families: the family I was born into, the family of friends and mentors I found here in America, and the family that makes up Define American. Many members of my families are recognized throughout this book, and you can meet my entire Define American family, including our board of trustees and advisory board, at defineamerican.com/team. My eternal thanks to the earliest supporters and champions of Define American, particularly Barbara Picower of the JPB Foundation, Taryn Higashi of Unbound Philanthropy, Cathy Cha of the Evelyn and Walter

Haas Jr. Fund, and Liz Simons of the Heising-Simons Foundation. Thank you to Ryan Eller for your leadership and the grace in which you exhibit it. Thank you, Jonathan Yu, for always being my first editor.

Teaching is a sacred profession to me, and educators have played a central role in my life. As I was writing this book, I thought of every teacher I ever had: Mrs. Mitchell and Ms. Girsky. Mrs. Fitzgerald, Mrs. Wakefield, Mrs. Furman, and Mrs. Thompson. Mrs. Nelson. Mrs. Fuqua. Mr. Zehner. Dr. Thornburg and Mrs. Dewar. Mr. Lee, Ms. Dorman, Mr. Farrell. Mrs. Denny. I will never forget them.

Arguably the biggest honor of my life is the opening of Jose Antonio Vargas Elementary School in my hometown of Mountain View, California. Tamara Wilson, a member of the local school board, suggested that the school be named after me. Dr. Ayinde Rudolph, the superintendent of the Mountain View Whisman School District, guided the process, with input from community members. Dr. Michael Jones will serve as the school's principal. I am thankful to each of them. It is thrilling to think that among the first readers of this book will be the teachers, parents, and students of the elementary school.

ABOUT THE AUTHOR

JOSE ANTONIO VARGAS, a journalist and filmmaker, is the founder and CEO of the nonprofit Define American. His work has appeared internationally in *Time*, as well as in the *San Francisco Chronicle*, the *New Yorker*, and the *Washington Post*, where he won a Pulitzer Prize as part of a reporting team. In 2014, he received the Freedom to Write Award from PEN Center USA. He directed the documentary feature *Documented* and MTV special *White People*, which was nominated for an Emmy Award. An elementary school named after him will open in his hometown of Mountain View, California, in 2019. You can visit him online at www.joseantoniovargas.com.